SIMPLY
FENG SHUI
FOR HOME, OFFICE & GARDEN

THE
COMPLETE
WORKING
TOOL

NORTH · YANG/YIN · BLACK WATER · BLUE EARTH · EAST · YIN/YANG · GREEN WOOD · PURPLE WOOD · YANG/YIN · SOUTH · RED FIRE · EARTH PINK · YIN/YANG · WEST · METAL WHITE · METAL GREY

WENDY HOBSON

foulsham
LONDON • NEW YORK • TORONTO • SYDNEY

foulsham

The Publishing House, Bennetts Close,
Cippenham, Berkshire, SL1 5AP, England

ISBN 0-572-02421-5

Printed in Great Britain by St. Edmundsbury Press, Bury St Edmunds

Contents

Introduction

From being the sole and secret preserve of the ancient Chinese emperors, the art of feng shui has become popular throughout both the Eastern and the Western worlds. Perhaps as a reaction against the speed of change which is endemic in modern society as it hurtles towards the twenty-first century, people have become aware of a lack of balance both in society as a whole and also perhaps in their own lives, and have turned to such ancient principles as feng shui in the hope of finding some redress to that imbalance and a way of restoring the harmony and structure of their lives.

Whether you already believe in the power of feng shui to create harmony and balance in your life, or whether you merely have a passing interest and want to find out more, the aim of this book is to provide a straightforward pathway towards a basic understanding of a very complex and highly structured philosophy. No one could hope to understand the entire meaning of feng shui and put all its principles into practice without the years of study and depth of intuitive understanding of the feng shui masters. Hopefully, however, this step-by-step guide will help set a firm foundation in your mind for your understanding of the subject and give you detailed and practical guidance on how to implement the principles of feng shui in your home environment in order to make your life happier and more fulfilling.

So why should you consider making lifestyle changes according to the principles of this ancient art? To answer this question, you could first look at the feng shui capital of the world, Hong Kong, and consider the continuing success of the former colony, despite the most far-reaching political changes over the latter part of the twentieth century. Or you could think about the success of the likes of the Richard Branson empire, the Harvey Nichols store and the Midland Bank, all of which apply feng shui principles to their working environments. If you succeed in making just a few changes in your home which create better harmony and balance in your environment, you can only benefit; there is nothing to lose and potentially everything to gain.

You probably already know that feng shui often uses symbolic motifs to implement its principles. Don't be put off by those who ridicule some of these symbolic gestures. They might ask how you can expect to win the lottery just by keeping the toilet lid down and the bathroom door shut. The answer, of course, is that you do not. You could counter that type of question and encourage them to be more open-minded about the implications of feng shui by asking whether they would choose to build a house on a flat and open plain raked by chilling winds, or one balanced on the precipice of a bare mountainside. They would be hard put not to agree that these descriptions of the worst positions in feng shui terms also coincide both with common sense, and with their own instinctive feelings about the most auspicious energies which should surround a home.

In all our lives, what we aim to achieve is a balance, a sense of harmony both within ourselves and with our surroundings. Feng shui can help you to do this. By thinking about the energies within you and around you, and making constructive changes to create beneficial effects in the movement of those energies, you will make changes in your life by actively affecting your own good fortune, rather than hanging around on the off chance that good luck will come to you.

Some of those changes will be logical ones, known in Chinese as *ru-shr*. Bringing a light or mirror into a dark hallway to make it more welcoming and lively really needs no mystical interpretation; it is common sense. You'll find there is a great deal of common sense in feng shui and it is important that you never lose sight of it. Other solutions may not stand up to the same logical examination; they may be *chu-shr*, mystical solutions. Painting a room in the south-western sector of a house yellow to enhance the prospects of a new relationship in your life cannot be judged by the same practical principles, but its effect may be even greater in changing your life.

How to use this book

As I have said, feng shui is an ancient and immensely complex art, and it is made of up a number of interconnecting facets, all of which have their unique ways of relating to one another – rather like the children's construction game in which you create three-dimensional structures with two-dimensional octagonal shapes by slotting them together. In addition, you will find when reading about the subject that different schools of feng shui and different masters will apply their own interpretations to sets of circumstances – very confusing for the beginner if their grounding in the basics is rocky.

Understanding these interrelationships need not be difficult, however, if you appreciate the basic principles underlying feng shui, and communicating these principles is what this book sets out to achieve. It is structured in such a way that it will guide you through the elements one by one, making sure that you understand and can apply the principles of the first topic before you move on to find out about the next, how it relates to the first, and how to apply what you have learned.

The order in which information is presented varies tremendously in different studies, indicating both the personal nature of the study and the fact that different practitioners give more priority to one element rather than another, and also that many aspects are of equal importance and need to be understood together. The concepts here are presented in such a way that the chapters do not leave questions unresolved. Occasionally a topic is drawn to your attention in brief before it is examined in more detail.

There are worksheets at the end of most of the chapters, on which you can draw or write any information you feel may be useful. That way, all your reference information will be safely in one place and there is no chance that even the most untidy will lose that slip of paper containing crucial information, or that even the most forgetful will need to work out their lucky compass directions for a third time. Rather than making lists or filling in forms, they are designed so that you draw your floor plans directly on to the templates provided, aligning them with the correct compass directions, and write around the plan any changes or improvements you want to make.

The other major advantage of creating a developing record is that as your understanding grows and the subject falls into place, you may well want to amend or adjust decisions you made earlier. Taking a measured and steady path, making significant changes rather than sweeping ones and finding compromises, if necessary, with partners and family is the right way to proceed and the most likely to succeed in making improvements in your life.

Changing your life

So how can feng shui change your life? With feng shui, you are not randomly choosing a set of lottery numbers which may or may not bring you luck. You are structuring your life around a series of tried-and-tested principles so that all the energies within and around you are aligned in a harmonious balance. Having achieved that, opportunities for good fortune are more likely to open up to you, and you will find that you are in a position to recognise and grasp them. Also, if bad luck comes your way – and it can never be totally within our control – you will be in a better position to cope with it. Feng shui is a way of encouraging you to be observant about your environment and to reflect on the ways it influences your life, and the ways you influence your surroundings. It is not a set of restrictive rules by which you contain your life; it should be looked upon as a set of guiding principles to help you put yourself in the best possible position in relation to the life forces of the universe so that you can get the maximum benefit in your life and minimise the down-sides.

Keep an open mind and consider carefully all the elements of feng shui as they are outlined to you. Use the worksheet pages to keep a record of your progress so that you do not have to keep going over the same ground. Think about your objectives and what you hope to achieve, then proceed in a measured and relaxed way to implement changes which will make a real difference to your life – for the better.

CHAPTER 1

What is Feng Shui?

An ancient and mystical art, the practice of feng shui has continued unbroken for thousands of years, putting into effect its blend of ancient wisdom and cultural superstition.

The development of feng shui

Legend has it that the sage Fu Hsi lived, more than three thousand years ago, in an area of China which was prone to flooding. One day, while meditating on the banks of the river Lo, he saw a turtle, the Chinese symbol of lifelong happiness, climb out of the river. He noticed that the patterns on the shell of the turtle were arranged in groups of numbers which created the *lo shu*, a magic square – a square in which all the numbers add up to fifteen in any direction. He believed that there are eight major types of energy in nature in addition to *tai ch'i*, the source and focus of all energies. Since the pattern on the turtle shell also had nine divisions, he concluded that they related to the same types of

energy which were, in fact, pervading everything in the universe. He allocated a trigram – a symbolic group of three lines – to each of the energies except *tai ch'i*.

Applying the principle that everything related to the same types of energy, he made improvements to the landscape which prevented the flooding and turned a difficult situation there into a prosperous one. He also developed the *I Ching*, the Chinese book of changes, in which he discussed and explained the wisdom and nature of change and offered guidance on every possible variation in the energies of the universe. It is on these foundations that feng shui is built. Literally meaning 'wind and water', it is a system by which every aspect of nature can be placed in harmony.

Originally the practice of feng shui remained the closely guarded secret of the emperors of China, who followed the dictates of their feng shui masters in the location and arrangement of their palaces and, most importantly, the location of the grave sites of their ancestors. The ancient Chinese – and to a lesser extent also the modern Chinese – revered and respected their ancestors. Locating a grave site in such a way that it would enable the living to benefit from the benign influences exerted by the dead was of primary importance to the ancient nobles. Keeping that information to themselves meant that others could not benefit to the same degree and therefore would pose less of a threat to their power. In fact, it has been said that the first Ming emperor actually spread misinformation on how to benefit from feng shui in order to confuse and cause the downfall of potential enemies.

Like any secret which is worth knowing, however, the emperors found that they were unable to keep all the benefits of feng shui to themselves, and gradually the practice of the art spread to the aristocracy and then further into the general population. The fact that its use has continued over thousands of years right up to modern times must be a testament to its effectiveness. The Communist Chinese leader Mao Tse Tung – while he believed in its principles and studied how it related to the successes and failures of previous rulers – nonetheless banned feng shui in China. The result of this was, of course, that it began to flourish in other Eastern cultures, notably in Taiwan where the former leader Chiang Kai Shek had taken many ancient feng shui documents as well as feng shui masters themselves. From there, Western countries have gradually come to learn about and embrace the concepts of feng shui.

Restoring the balance

The basic aim of feng shui is simplicity itself: to enhance the quality of life by ensuring that you are living in harmony with the forces of nature. This little story illustrates the basis of how it begins to work. In a mountainous district of China, a family were living in a small house perched precariously on the mountainside. The son's room overlooked the towering, rocky mountainside; the daughter's room on the opposite side looked out over the valley, the steep rocks falling away beneath the window. The son often felt depressed and confused; he felt

that he could not move forward towards what he wanted to achieve in life, but was always blocked at every turn by obstacles in his path. The daughter, on the other hand, suffered from feelings of insecurity and lack of stability; she would move from one project to the next, never quite finding a secure base.

Worried by the fact that their children's behaviour was unstable, the parents called in the feng shui master to offer solutions to the problems. He defined the environmental influences which were strongest on each of the children. The son was oppressed by the dark, solid rocks, while the daughter could see the land slipping away beneath her. Balance needed to be restored to their environment. So he planted bamboo behind the house to block the view of the mountainside, introducing lightness and movement to the son's view and bringing wood symbols of growth and progress. Then at the front of the house, he arranged for a balcony to be built, with a strong barrier and potted plants to give a horizontal view from the girl's window. By applying a sense of balance to the environment, he was able to alter the perceptions and the state of mind of the youngsters and allow them to feel more comfortable and to begin to have a more positive outlook.

Making your own luck

By restoring the natural balance in yourself and in your surroundings and creating favourable energy around your home, you establish the right environment for improving every aspect of your life. Living in a balanced environment eliminates stress and fosters good health. Being at ease with yourself helps to encourage good relationships with family, friends and other people who cross your path in life. The respect which that engenders creates opportunities in the social sphere for fulfilling relationships and enjoying a fortunate life. In the business world, it creates opportunities for growth, advancement and prosperity.

Feng shui does this by stimulating one of the three kinds of good fortune, or luck. We are all influenced by *tien chai*, heaven luck, with which we are born and which is outside our control. The study of Chinese astrology can give more understanding of your *tien chai* and how to cope with it. Feng shui focuses on strengthening your earth luck, *ti chai:* the luck which responds to your environment, brings changes and improves your chances of success. However, this can only reach its maximum potential when supported by *ren chai*, mankind luck, the luck you create for yourself by seizing the opportunities which *ti chai* brings. Unlike waiting to win the lottery, you have to take an active part in making your own luck if you really want to get the best out of your life.

CHAPTER 2

Understanding Ch'i

The first thing to understand when thinking about feng shui is the concept of ch'i. Ch'i is sometimes translated as the breath of life or the dragon's breath. A subtle flow of electromagnetic energy, it permeates everything in the universe. The ideal way in which this breath of life moves through the universe is in a smooth, moderate, meandering and untroubled manner.

The three kinds of luck are related to the three basic kinds of ch'i. *Tien ch'i*, heaven ch'i, is governed by the heavens and is outside our control. *Ti ch'i* is contained in the veins of the earth and it is because of *ti ch'i* that we are influenced by the landscape and by our environment. *Ren ch'i* moves between the fixed heaven and earth, carried in the wind and water. The Chinese symbolise the earth as the body of the dragon and the streams and waterways as the dragon's blood; both carry ch'i around the universe.

As we have seen, feng shui means 'wind and water'. Water, *shui*, is the sustainer of life without which nothing can exist. The movement of air, the wind or *feng*, acts as a carrier for the water and is equally essential to survival. As well as being contained in the landscape, therefore, the wind and water also carry across the earth with them this subtle flow of electromagnetic energy.

To find the most auspicious environment in which to live means identifying the place where the *ti ch'i* is at its best. For most of us, this means looking at where we already live, assessing the positive and negative elements of the environmental ch'i and taking measures to optimise the benefits. The principles and methods used to achieve this are known as the form school of feng shui.

Helping the movement of free-flowing ch'i is the next stage, and we will move on to look at how to identify ch'i movement, do away with negative influences and generally improve its flow.

The ideal movement of ch'i

Science has proved to us that all matter is a manifestation of types of energy and we arrange our lives around the organisation of real objects which are, in fact, made up of different kinds of energy. Ch'i is also a type of energy, but an invisible one, no less potent for the fact that we cannot see it in the same way as the solid objects with which we are surrounded.

Ch'i circulates around the entire universe, through everything from the tiniest insect, through humans and their environment. Every element of life is interlinked and interdependent and ch'i is the linking force which flows through everything. Everyone has, at one time or another, dropped a pebble into the waters of a puddle and watched the ripples spreading across the surface – a small cause having a great effect. The other classic example of the same phenomenon is the butterfly moving its wings on one side of the globe and causing a hurricane on the other. We do not have to understand the laws of physics fully to see that action and interaction, cause and effect are linked in the physical world.

Similarly, they are linked in the invisible world. If one person in a group of happy and lively people is feeling depressed and unhappy, they will feel out of balance with the general mood of the gathering. In the same way, if one energy is moving through every aspect of the universe, we need to be in balance and harmony with that energy in order to feel at peace. Our own feelings – the way the ch'i flows through our bodies – affects our surroundings. The ch'i flowing through our surroundings affects how we are feeling. If there is an imbalance either way, then we feel tense and uncomfortable. This can easily be demonstrated if you think about walking through an unfamiliar and perhaps aggressive neighbourhood, then compare that feeling with walking down your own street. Out of harmony with your surroundings, you are uncomfortable or stressed; in balance, you feel relaxed. Making a change in that environment – in this instance, moving from the unfamiliar and aggressive to the familiar and friendly – affects the way we feel in quite a radical way.

This is where feng shui can help. By taking positive action to change those elements which are clearly out of balance, we can use that interaction to our advantage. We can change our surroundings to improve the way we feel about ourselves and our immediate environment which, in itself, will create other changes in our lives. The effect is just like the ripples on the pond. So if we can learn to live in harmony with our environment and blend with the natural landscape, that can only be to our advantage.

Ch'i in the body – the chakras

The first exercise in moving towards harmony with your environment is to ensure that the energy flow through your own body is smooth. Ch'i flows through the human body along energy lines known as meridians and focuses on seven energy centres or chakras. These are positioned on the top of the head, between the eyes, at the throat, the heart, the solar plexus, the navel and the groin.

Each chakra is associated with a particular part of the body and an area of our lives; it is also sympathetic to a colour. The crown chakra at the top of the head controls our destiny and everything to do with the brain. It relates to the colour purple. The third eye chakra, between the eyes, is the centre of intuition and psychic insight. From a physical point of view, it is associated with the ears, nose and throat and it is associated with the colour indigo. The centre of our identity and creativity is the throat chakra; the colour with which it is associated is blue. Physical or health issues relate to the throat or neck. In the centre of the chest, the heart chakra vibrates to the colour green.

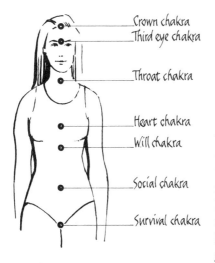

Crown chakra
Third eye chakra
Throat chakra
Heart chakra
Will chakra
Social chakra
Survival chakra

The love we have for ourselves and for others emanates from this point, which connects us all as living things. Both physically and emotionally, it rules the chest and the heart. The will chakra is positioned in the solar plexus and is associated with the colour yellow. The stomach, liver and other associated organs are implicated in the health aspects of this chakra, while on a spiritual level it controls our intellect and will: the direction we choose to take in life. Just below the navel, the social chakra controls the emotions, sexual energy and self-esteem. Orange is its related colour, and physical issues dealing with the lower intestines and lower back are appropriate here. Finally, the survival chakra is found at the base of the spine and resonates to the colour red. Related to money and survival, it controls the genitals, legs and feet.

Relaxation and meditation

If the energy is flowing smoothly through the energy meridians in the body, you will feel relaxed, healthy and energised. If not, or if the energies associated with any of the individual chakras are out of balance, you will feel weak and depressed because ch'i strengthens and energises the body. Those who practise acupressure, acupuncture and reflexology use those meridians to stimulate the body's energy for healing. Students of oriental martial arts learn the ability to concentrate the ch'i in order to perform sometimes amazing feats.

In normal daily life, you do not necessarily need either of these extremes, but keeping the bodily energies in balance does reduce stress and promote good health and general well-being. Simple methods of relaxation or meditation are the best ways to achieve this and different people will find different methods more appropriate to them; the only important thing is that you completely relax your body and your mind – forget entirely about work, shopping and all the million other things you have to do.

Some people will be able to achieve that level of relaxation by soaking in a hot lavender bath listening to soothing music. Others may have to use other ways of relaxing or meditating. If you are not used to relaxing completely, you may find that a physical approach suits you best. Lie comfortably in a warm room and make sure that you will not be disturbed. Starting with your feet, then your lower legs, then your thighs and working through each set of muscle groups in turn, clench the muscles as tightly as you can, hold for 10 seconds, then release. Work right through the body, including the face. As you feel the contrast between tension and relaxation, you will be able to relax completely and enjoy the sensation for as long as you wish. The concentration on your body will help to clear your mind of other trivia and allow you to let go completely. When you are ready, you can gradually allow your mind to wake up and think about what you need to be doing. It may take a little practice to become proficient in the technique but by that time you may not even need to go through the tensing and relaxing process; that is just a means to an end.

Another simple method is to concentrate on each of the chakras in turn, starting with the groin and working up to the crown chakra. Try to focus your mind on nothing but the energy centre in question, again clearing your mind of other extraneous information. You may even feel a tingling sensation as you proceed through the body – a sure sign that the chakras are being stimulated. Other meditation and visualisaton techniques are described in the many books on the subject.

Being able to release stress and relax is vitally important in our ever-more-complex lifestyles. You can visualise the effect as the ch'i flowing in a comfortable and meandering line through your body, rather than dashing from one point to the next, constantly changing direction or stagnating in dead ends. Even if you go no further with your feng shui, or you see this simply as a way of recharging your batteries rather than aligning yourself with universal principles, you will gain benefits from learning to relax – a good reason in itself to move on to the next stage.

Auras

Our personal ch'i is not confined strictly to the body but extends perhaps 30 cm/12 in outside the body in what is known as the aura. The extent and potency of different people's auras varies depending on their personality and how attuned they are to their bodily ch'i, so a person who meditates and whose ch'i aura is smooth will give off positive energies. As people interact in social situations, so their auras overlap and merge. Someone who is stressed, nervous and uncomfortable does not attract other people to relate to them; and if you are close to them you may find yourself feeling uncomfortable too – influenced by their mood and their aura. On the other hand, outgoing people with a stimulated ch'i tend to have a greater influence over the people around them.

Being in tune with your own ch'i flow – your own instinctive feelings if you like – will help you identify with others and relate to them. You will find that if you are more attuned to the ch'i in yourself, you will be more attuned to the ch'i in others and also to the ch'i in your general surroundings, the ultimate purpose of feng shui.

CHAPTER 3

Harnessing the Power of the Four Celestial Animals

The universe and everything within it pulsates to the energies of ch'i flowing through it. The most straightforward feng shui, the form school, deals with how we find the most auspicious places to live so that we are in harmony with the universal ch'i. The importance of symbolism in Chinese culture has also already been mentioned, so it will come as no suprise that, as well as the dragon, there are three more celestial animals which have a strong symbolic significance in feng shui.

The four celestial animals

In the form school of feng shui, the shape of the landscape is considered vital to locating the most auspicious luck, and the shape of that landscape is linked to the symbolic nature of the four celestial animals: the dragon, the tiger, the turtle and the phoenix.

The dragon

The dragon is the most potent symbol in Chinese tradition and is viewed in a number of different ways. The whole landscape is often described as the body of the dragon, and dragons themselves are said to live in undulating mountain ranges as they will not live in flat or barren landscapes. They are the ultimate symbol of good luck, bringing prosperity and abundance. It follows that in looking for an auspicious environment in which to live, the area must have some hills of moderate height in order to ensure that those living there can rely on the positive influence of the dragon.

Hills have the added effect of helping the correct movement of ch'i through the air, as completely flat plains or very windy sites encourage the ch'i to move too quickly, another reason to look for a landscape of hills rather than a flat area.

There are other qualities of the dragon, as well as the other celestial animals, which will be fully explained in later chapters. One of these is the concept of yin and yang; these two opposing but complementary forces of energy are discussed on pages 37–43. The dragon is regarded as a male symbol and, as such, its energy is wholly yang. He is associated with the compass direction east, which is linked with the season of spring and the colour dark green. He is therefore often referred to as the green dragon.

The tiger

Symbolising protection, the tiger's strength should always be second to that of the dragon, exercising a containing rather than a controlling influence. Tiger hills, as you would expect, are therefore lower and more rounded than dragon hills. To achieve perfect harmony, both dragon and tiger must be in evidence in the environment.

Since the dragon is male, the tiger – as its balancing opposite – is therefore female and relates to yin. Her compass direction is the west and her related season is the autumn. The symbolic colour of the tiger is white, and she is often known as the white tiger.

The turtle

The turtle symbolises support, stability and longevity. Lower, rounded hills – shaped like the back of the turtle shell – represent the qualities of the turtle and will enhance the lifestyle of those living near them in the same ways. Again, this emphasises a moderate landscape, not entirely flat but with rolling hills offering support and protection.

The compass direction related to the turtle is the north. It is linked with the winter and the colour black.

The phoenix

The phoenix is the last of the four celestial animals. The new creature rising from its own ashes is a potent symbol of opportunity, grasping and making the best of circumstances which arise. Low hillocks, in balance with the three other types of hill, represent the presence of the phoenix in the landscape.

Red is the colour of fire and of the phoenix, whose compass direction is the south and whose associated season is the summer.

The ideal home site

If each of the four celestial animals is represented in the landscape around your home, then the signs are positive that it will be an auspicious site. However, it is important that the animals – or their symbolic representations – are in the correct balance and in the ideal positions. In looking for an ideal site, *hseuh*, you would therefore look for a very specific arrangement of hills and plains.

For the ancient Chinese, these symbolic representations meant, quite literally, the shape of the hills surrounding the potential home site, and for some people that may still be the case. For urban dwellers, however, ranges of hills of different character are more than a little irrelevant. All we need to do, however, is to remember that we are thinking symbolically and trying to encourage the correct flow of ch'i energy. Ch'i can be channelled or influenced by any physical object – whether that happens to be a hill or a building – so we can look at our surroundings in exactly the same way, considering the lie of the land overall but also the buildings in the immediate surroundings.

Since the dragon is the most potent symbol, dragon hills are crucial for good feng shui, and a home nestling near the heart and belly of the dragon is the best place of all. The dragon hills, or higher buildings, should ideally be on the left side of the house, looking out from the main door. Opposite, on the right side of the house to balance the dragon, should be lower tiger hills. If these two ranges of hills are in a horseshoe shape and merge together behind the site, this symbolic copulation of the two celestial animals is highly auspicious.

For maximum support, the position of the turtle should be behind the house; the backrest on a symbolic armchair in which the dragon and tiger hills provide the armrests and the home site nestles on the seat. The only animal to position, then, is the phoenix, which becomes the footstool in the front of the house. The land should slope away gently from the front of the house to these low hills, rather than the house being below the level of the land in front.

So if we were trying to locate the ideal feng shui site on which to build our dream home, we would look for a gently hilly area. The place for the house would be with low hills to the right and a higher range to the left. Rounded hills or structures behind the site and a more open plain with small hillocks in front complete the picture. The hills provide an undulating landscape rather than a flat one and encourage a balance of sun and shade. Winds are able to move easily around the area in a gentle motion. All these elements encourage a lush vegetation and no damp or stagnant areas.

The position of water is also important in the perfect home, as ideally a flowing river should meander in an arc across the front of the plot. Because water is so important in the movement of ch'i, we will look at that in more detail later in the book.

Now relate this ideal site to an urban environment. You are probably already becoming familiar and more comfortable with the way the symbolism works and automatically starting to relate to your own surroundings.

For the perfect site, the taller, dragon buildings or trees should be on the left – looking out from the main door – with the smaller buildings on the right, both offering protection. It is best to have some higher buildings behind the house to offer support, rather than an open area. The front of the house, on the other hand, should be more open, not hemmed in by taller structures which are too close and block out the phoenix of opportunity.

The river is represented in the urban environment by a road; this will be explained in detail later. As the river in front should be meandering and free-flowing but neither too fast nor too sluggish, this translates as a medium-sized road with some traffic but neither fast-moving cars constantly rushing past the house nor traffic jams bringing the flow to a standstill.

Assessing your home

If these ideal situations exactly describe the position of your home, then you are fortunate, as you are in the best possible place to maximise the

ti chai. This will clearly not be the case for everyone, however, so this is the point at which we begin to make positive changes to our situation to come as near as possible to the ideal.

Start to fill in the information you discover on the worksheet pages so that you can use it to make gradual and considered changes in and around your home. Do not expect to act on everything at once. You may want to make small changes based on your conclusions at each stage, gradually adding to and amending the changes as you go along, or you may want to start an overall plan which will grow as you work through the book. Either way, proceeding with understanding and caution is the most effective way.

Drawing a sketch

The first thing to do is to stand outside in front of your house looking at your front door and use the space on page 28 to make a very rough sketch of what you see. It does not matter if you cannot draw to save your life – the idea of actually putting something down on paper is to make you look really closely at how your property relates to those around it, and that is all your sketch needs to indicate. The lines only need to be accurate enough to remind you of the type of shapes – rounded, pointed, square – and the relationship between the objects – whether they are larger or smaller than your property and in which direction they are positioned.

Completing the worksheet

For most people, the use of urban terminology is appropriate, and this is what is used from now on in the book. For those who live surrounded by actual mountains, the assessment is even easier so you can forgive the fact that the text talks about buildings and roads instead of hills.

Look at the drawing you have made and write down whether you feel the symbolic representations of the individual celestial animals are missing, in the correct balance, too predominant or not sufficiently dominant. Think about the symbolism of the celestial animals and look at your home in a new way. Does it have the support of the turtle behind? Are the buildings higher on the left or the right? Is it blocked at the front or can you see the open space and low hillocks of the phoenix footstool? Are any of the elements missing altogether? Also write down the direction of the land slope in front of your house, whether it slopes down towards the main door or down away from it.

Establishing your home's compass directions

Having this picture of your own property in your mind will make it easier to understand this next section, which deals with restoring the situation to make it as close as possible to the ideal.

In general terms, you can continue to relate the position of the celestial animals to their position on the left, right, behind or in front of your property. However, if you need extra help, you may want to energise those sections of the home which relate to the compass directions linked with each animal: the turtle in the north; the phoenix in the south; the dragon in the east; and the tiger in the west. To do this, you will need to know the compass directions from the main door of your home.

The Chinese compass

It is traditional in Chinese work to depict the compass with the south at the top, and this is how it will be shown in this book so that you get used to seeing things in that way; this will help when you read other books on the subject and you will quickly become used to it. This does not affect the compass directions. They all relate to the magnetic compass directions which you can take from any ordinary compass.

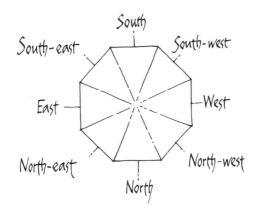

To ascertain the direction in which your property faces, stand at your front door and take the compass directions. Write down the direction in which both your front and back doors face; you will be using them all the time from now on.

Replacing missing celestial animals

If you live in an isolated property in a flat landscape, this is not good feng shui. However, by definition, it also means that you have the space to stimulate perfect feng shui around your home. Since this requires some fairly drastic action, you can make an overall plan, then implement it gradually, depending on which areas of your life you most wish to improve or to stimulate.

The dragon

The dragon is the most powerful symbol and represents abundance and prosperity. If your life is running along fairly smoothly or if you feel you want help in every aspect of your life, this is the area on which to concentrate. Don't be without the beneficial influence of the dragon in your life. Making sure that you always allow plenty of space for the ch'i to flow around the house and, not positioning any plants or buildings too near to it, think about erecting a fence or planting a hedge or trees on the left-hand side of the house to stimulate the energies of the dragon.

In the meantime, or if you prefer a less challenging solution – since the dragon is so vital to your general good fortune – you can energise his qualities by placing a picture or statue of a dragon in the eastern part of your home, the area relating to the dragon. The living room is a good place for this as it is the centre of the family's activity; the bedroom is not an auspicious position as the active energies are too strong for a place of sleep and relaxation. The image should not be too large, otherwise it will be overpowering and therefore stressful, but it must show a fat and contented animal. Choose an image of a four-clawed dragon; avoid the five-clawed imperial dragon whose influence is too strong. If you overstimulate the dragon, an aggressive atmosphere can result and you will know that you have gone too far.

The tiger

Protection is offered by the tiger, but always in balance with the dragon. Once you have supplied the dragon, add a smaller hedge or collection of shrubs to the right-hand side of the building. You can try introducing an image of a white tiger into the west side of the house – either a statue or a picture – but take care that the tiger is never given more prominence than the dragon otherwise this can exert a malevolent influence over the property.

The turtle

If you feel that it is the support of the turtle you are lacking, then you need to position a taller, preferably rounded structure or shape behind the house. Again, perhaps a fence or hedge can supply the deficiency, or you may even be able to create a hillock at the back of the garden. It does not have to be huge; remember that we are working symbolically. If this is not possible, you can introduce a bronze turtle into the garden to provide the support. In the *lo shu* square on the back of the turtle, the number one appears in the northerly position at the bottom of the shell. The turtle relates to the north and therefore also to the number one, so one turtle in the garden is quite enough. You may, of course, be lucky enough to have a real animal, which would be even better. If there are no other options, place a statue or a picture of a single turtle in the northern part of your house.

The phoenix

A low fence or hedge, a row of small shrubs or even a garden statue at the front of the house can stimulate the phoenix of opportunity. Make sure you allow plenty of free space in front of the house. This space is needed for the ch'i to settle and accumulate before it moves into your home. Keep the space open and the symbolic hills subtle. If you choose a statue, you might find it hard to buy a phoenix, but other red birds – a rooster or a flamingo, for example – will take its place just as well. If you choose to stimulate the energy with a picture of one of these birds, place it in the southern part of the house.

The celestial animals out of balance

In most cases, especially in towns and villages, homes do have surrounding properties and it is more likely that while the celestial animals are all represented, their positions or size mean that they are out of balance. Using similar principles to those acted upon to replace any missing animals, this can be rectified to improve the feng shui of your home and its surroundings.

The dragon

As we have seen, dragons are essential to good feng shui. Without the influence of the dragon, you will find that you are lacking in the energy to take control of your life and you may suffer from bad luck in all areas, which you will rarely attribute to your own attitude of mind.

If there are no buildings on the left of your property or they are much smaller than those on the right and therefore their influence is not sufficiently dominant, you need to redress the balance. Look at the previous section on supplying an absent dragon by erecting a fence or planting a hedge or trees, or placing an image of the dragon in the eastern sector of the home.

If the dragon is too dominant, then his influence will encourage overstimulation which can lead to stress and even aggression; male members of the family may become disproportionately important in the group. If the situation is caused by tall trees or something which you can change, think about whether you would like to prune them down or replace them with smaller trees or a hedge. Remember that you must maintain the influence of the dragon, not do away with it altogether. If the situation is created by buildings or something else which cannot be altered, then you will need to introduce more strength to the tiger element so that a balance between them is re-established. Look back to the previous section on how to do this.

The tiger

As we have seen, the tiger must be in balance with the dragon. If she is missing altogether or too subservient, you can add a low hedge, a fence or shrubs. If you want to stimulate the tiger within the home, introduce a tiger ornament or image in the west of the house or the western side of the living room.

On the other hand, if the tiger is too dominant, she will have a malevolent influence on your luck. If you can reduce the size of trees to the right of the house, that will help. If you cannot do this, introduce a spotlight on the right-hand side to illuminate the area. This has the effect of stimulating the yang associated with the dragon to counterbalance the yin of the tiger.

The turtle

If the turtle is missing or not sufficiently prominent, you can add trees at the back of the house to provide the necessary support, or perhaps do some landscaping in the garden to create a rounded hillock. Otherwise, add a symbolic turtle in the north, as outlined on page 25.

If the buildings at the back of the house are so dominant as to be overpowering and oppressive, you need to counter this by breaking their influence. Plant some bamboo to provide a screen of lighter, upward-moving wood to counter the over-strong influence, or hang a crystal in the window to activate the positive energies and deflect any negative ones.

The phoenix

Replacing a missing element here can be very subtle. Introduce a low fence or hedge, or plant a few shrubs at the front of your garden, or set up a statue to represent the phoenix – as we have seen, a flamingo or a rooster can be substituted – to provide the benefit of the celestial bird's influence.

It is ideal if the slope at the front of the house goes down away from your front door. If your house is below the level of the road or land in front, it can mean that your life feels lacking in foundation. To rectify this, raise the threshold of the property by about 5 cm/2 in so that you step over the threshold into the house.

Completing the worksheet

Now return to the worksheet and relate these feng shui solutions to any problems you recognise on your own home site. Think about how you can achieve the perfect balance and take steps to begin to change your life for the better.

My Home Site

*Sketch of home in relation to the surrounding hills,
buildings or trees*

THE DRAGON IS

THE TIGER IS

THE TURTLE IS

THE PHOENIX IS

THE LAND AT THE FRONT SLOPES

FRONT DOOR FACES

BACK OF THE HOUSE FACES

ACTION REQUIRED

CHAPTER 4

Directing the Flow of Ch'i

We have established that the ideal flow of ch'i, the subtle current of electromagnetic energy through all things, is with a measured and meandering movement. Relaxation and meditation can enhance that style of ch'i movement through the body. We also need to provide the circumstances for ch'i to have a similar relaxed beneficial flow through the environment. Visualise the energy passing in and around your home and your surroundings; think in symbolic terms and you will easily see how the system is meant to work.

Picture in your mind's eye a youthful river dashing headlong over rocks or down steep cliffs and crashing over boulders. It is moving quickly, constantly changing direction, regularly hitting obstacles headlong and being thrown off course. Its mood is angry and aggressive; there is so much energy that much of it is being misdirected and wasted. If ch'i moves in this way it is known as *sha ch'i*, and is not conducive to contented living. It acts just like a knife, cutting through positive energies so that at best it reduces their effectiveness and at worst it destroys them altogether.

Now think about the river at the end of its course to the ocean, where it becomes sluggish and heavy with debris. It curves so widely and slowly across its flat flood plain that it begins to stagnate at the apex of its wide bends. Ch'i likened to this is *si ch'i*, too weak and depressed to offer auspicious surroundings. A house influenced by too much *si ch'i* is likely to find the occupants lethargic and apathetic, lacking in drive and energy.

Finally, visualise the river making its progress through the centre of its course. It is moving steadily across a meandering plain; several tributaries are joining it along its path. There is constant rhythmic movement, an uninterrupted forward motion through smooth-flowing curves, giving the water enough power gently to surround or avoid obstacles in its path without confrontation or deflection from its logical course. It has the controlled power to maintain its chosen direction and speed. This is *sheng ch'i*, the breath of a contented dragon and what feng shui aims to achieve. There are more aspects to creating perfect *sheng ch'i*, which we will explain in other chapters, but the correct movement of ch'i in relation to the home is the single most important factor in aligning our surroundings auspiciously with the energy lines. If your home allows the ch'i to circulate gently, accumulate and rest without stagnating, you will have the best opportunities for a harmonious life.

Water, roads and ch'i flow

One of the main channels of ch'i in the landscape is water and in urban feng shui, this translates to the roads surrounding your property. The water courses and roads act as conduits which disperse ch'i through and around the region.

Since water is associated with wealth in Chinese symbolism, clearly the best way for water or roads to pass your house is in a meandering route, flowing neither too fast so that money rushes straight past you, nor too slowly so that it does not bring prosperity. If a house is facing a busy road, a motorway or a raised road, the occupants could find themselves unable to hold on to money. Their financial situation may fluctuate as money streams in and out of their possession.

It is better if a house is positioned on a gently curving road with moderate traffic flow. A house built at a junction which resembles the confluence of a stream is well positioned as long as no *sha ch'i* is directed at the main door, as we will see in the next section. These houses indicate an accumulation of wealth for those living there.

Houses in a cul-de-sac benefit from a pooling of ch'i as it circulates around the close, although the house at the end should also look out for *sha ch'i* if the road is pointing directly at the front door. If there is a roundabout at the end of the cul-de-sac, however, this serves to direct the ch'i flow on to an auspicious path.

Correcting negative influences

The best way to rectify the problem of a fast-moving road is to erect a barrier to protect the home and create an area of calm in front of the door where the ch'i has a chance to settle before it enters the house. Low hedges or fences are the best way to achieve this. Other options are to raise the threshold by a few centimetres so that you have to step over a symbolic barrier preventing negative energies entering the house. If you are able to reposition the main door, or use another door as your front door, clearly that is a radical but effective solution.

Identifying sha ch'i

Negative ch'i, *sha ch'i*, is created when the energy is either channelled too quickly along a straight, narrow feature, or when it is focused by a sharp, angular or pointed structure. These straight lines have the power to cut through positive ch'i and reduce its beneficial effects. For the original feng shui masters, that may have meant a narrow river valley, a jagged mountain range or a sharp peak. For us, it means a straight road, the corner of a large building or a pointed roof. It is important to evaluate any *sha ch'i* affecting your home and take steps to minimise or eliminate any negative effects, since *sha ch'i* can destroy any other good feng shui actions you take to enhance your property. *Sha ch'i* is often known as cutting ch'i, or cutting, killing or secret arrows.

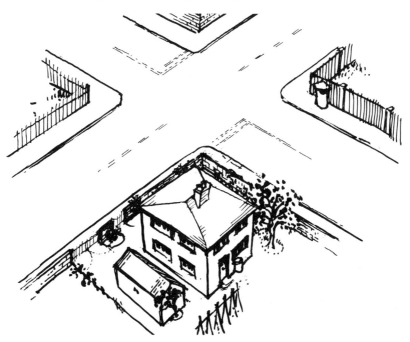

The primary source of *sha ch'i* is from straight roads running directly up to your home, particularly to your front door. Therefore if your house is directly opposite a T-junction or a sharp corner, is at the end of a dead end or stands at a sharp junction or crossroads, it will be affected by *sha ch'i*. Similarly, if one or more roads run directly towards the house at an angle, this creates *sha ch'i* and will have a negative effect on the occupants of the house. A narrow gap between tall buildings opposite the main door also creates a killing arrow directed towards the house.

Another source of killing arrows is where a pointed feature is directed at the house. This could be a tall tower, the corner of a building or an extension, exaggerated roof lines or the pointed eaves of a neighbouring house. Killing arrows are also created by satellite dishes, telephone wires, television aerials, antennae, lamp posts, flag poles, pylons or spires. Trees, particularly if they are unhealthy, directly opposite the main door can also be a source of negative energy.

To assess any *sha ch'i* affecting your home, stand at your front door and look out. Think about the direction of the roads and paths. Are there any killing arrows directed at you? Then look at specific features of the surrounding buildings and identify the source of any negative ch'i. Then you should look at any killing arrows directed at the back of the house or at the windows, especially the bedroom or living room window. You may, for example, have a road running up to the back of the house or a satellite dish pointing at the lounge window. All these will have negative effects which need to be addressed.

Correcting sha ch'i influences

Once you have identified any problems with *sha ch'i* influencing your home, you will need to consider what can be done to rectify the situation. There are a number of things you can do, one of which is bound to be appropriate to your situation. In every case, the principle of the action is to redirect the negative energy away from your home.

One of the first things which you may be able to do to correct a problem you have identified is to use a different door as your main door. Ch'i energy moves through everything and where there are people, there is a focus of ch'i energy. It follows that as people move in and out of a house through the main door, this is also where most of the ch'i enters the house. If a killing arrow is directed at the main door, it will be a negative rather than a positive energy having a major influence on the home. In this case, it may be possible to use a side or back door as your main door. If you are building or extending the property, it is worth considering changing the direction the main door faces, or you may be able to introduce a porch to deflect the negative energies.

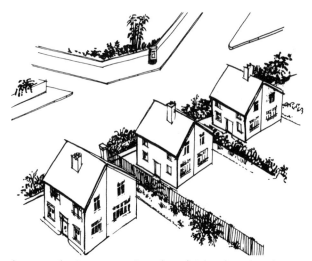

Obviously, these solutions can involve fairly drastic changes as they work by moving the door away from the killing arrows and will usually not be possible. There are plenty of simpler remedies which can be effective, however, and these work by deflecting the killing arrows themselves rather than moving the target. A hedge, a fence or a gate can be introduced to deflect the negative effects. They do not have to be

large structures which completely block out the bad influence, but can be quite small features. Small features can, in themselves, create *sha ch'i*, so don't choose a fence which looks like a row of pointed arrows or you may make things worse rather than better.

Another way to deflect *sha ch'i* is to hang a mirror on the outside of the house to reflect the energy back where it came from. A bagua mirror is particularly appropriate although this must only be used outside the house; you will find more details on page 89. When you place your mirror, make sure that the reflection is pointing somewhere harmless and not straight at a neighbour's door.

A fountain is an excellent way to deflect negative energies coming into the house and will benefit everyone in the building. There are no negative problems related to them. You can also use net curtains which allow in light but block out the negative energies.

If you have exceptionally powerful *sha ch'i* directed at your home from large neighbouring buildings, as a last resort you can use an image of crossed swords or a cannon, but these should only be used in extreme circumstances and you must be especially careful in which direction you deflect the negative energies.

Dealing with si ch'i

Si ch'i is not as great a problem as *sha ch'i* in your surroundings since its influence is negative rather than aggressive. However, areas where ch'i is stagnating mean that you are wasting potential energy and this can have a draining effect on your fortunes. Look for 'dead' corners around the house where you can visualise the energy finding a way into the space but not a way out.

The best way to energise these areas is to position plants or small statues to help to redirect the flow of energy into a more natural course. Plants will also nourish the ch'i, creating even more positive benefits.

The benefits of sheng ch'i

Establishing a good flow of ch'i around your home, *sheng ch'i*, will give you a more positive outlook on life and make you feel more in harmony with your surroundings. If good fortune comes your way, you will be in a better position to make the best of it. If, on the other hand, you experience some bad luck, you will be less likely to let it get you down and you will cope with the problem and move on. This more positive attitude will help you in every aspect of your life: your relationships, your career prospects and your general well-being and happiness.

Sha Ch'i and Si Ch'i Worksheet

Road going past the house

....

ACTION REQUIRED
....

SHA CH'I
....

ACTION REQUIRED
....

SI CH'I
....

ACTION REQUIRED

....

....

....

....

....

....

....

....

....

....

....

....

....

CHAPTER 5

Yin and Yang

All ch'i energy is qualified as yin or yang and the universe is a balance of these primordial, complementary yet opposing forces: the light, warm, masculine yang contrasting with the dark, cold, feminine yin. When they unite, they create *tao*, the principle which links man and the universe. Yin and yang each have their own attributes and magnetic fields of energy, but neither can exist alone. The traditional symbol of the universe divided into yin and yang illustrates how the polarities interact. The light half of the circle represents yang, but within it is the dark spot of yin energy. On the other side, the yin energy contains the light element of yang at its heart. *Tao* exists where yin and yang are in perfect balance.

The qualities of yang and yin

Yang is the energy of life and the energy of heaven. It is a positive, creative force which is characterised by light, warmth and sunshine. As a male force, it is impregnating, fiery and hard. Odd numbers are considered more yang. In the landscape, yang energy is found in hills rather than plains or valleys, and particularly in south-facing slopes. The summer is the predominantly yang season, with its brightness and activity. Yang is an expanding energy, full of motion and power.

Yin balances and opposes all these yang characteristics, the ultimate contrast being death as against life. Found in north-facing valleys, yin has the fertile qualities of the female and is dark, soft and nourishing. It offers a feeling of completion, thus even numbers are yin numbers. Winter is yin: cold and still. Its nature is yielding and quiet, characterised by moonlight and water rather than sunlight and fire.

As all matter contains elements of yin and yang, so these energies are also constantly in flux. Day changes to night, summer to winter, sunlight to moonlight, light to dark.

Achieving a balance

One of the aims of feng shui is to achieve a fundamental balance between the yin and the yang to provide the perfect atmosphere for whatever human activity is taking place. As a general rule, the yang energy of life should be the stronger, but should never be completely without its balancing yin element. Places where yin and yang are severely out of balance are bad places for humans to exist. Consider the desert regions of the world – the freezing, yin poles and the baking, yang deserts – neither of which offer hospitable environments.

Any building, whether it is a home, a garden or a workplace, needs a balance of yin and yang, and this should be tailored to suit the activities of the building or area, or any particular part of it. A harmony of opposites in the most auspicious proportions is what you are aiming for. In your living areas or workplace, the emphasis should be on yang to encourage high energy levels, activity and progress. In places you use for relaxation – bedrooms or quiet reading rooms, for example – you will want to accentuate the peace of the yin characteristics.

By virtue of their natural characteristics, people have a yin/yang balance within their own personality. The outgoing, energetic and bubbly yang person contrasts with the quiet, withdrawn, contemplative yin person. This will mean that the balance which is right for you is a personal one. A retiring person will not feel comfortable with too heavy an emphasis on yang and vice versa. On the other hand, introducing a little more of your opposite quality into the surroundings can have a beneficial effect, energising a sombre person or calming an overactive one.

The influence of the surroundings

The building itself will be influenced by its surroundings, which will alter the yin/yang balance. If your building is near any place which is symbolically associated with death or darkness – a graveyard, hospital, prison or police station or an empty area which was once used for buildings – it will have too heavy a yin influence. This can also be the case if the building has formerly been used for a similar activity or if it is heavily surrounded by tall trees and undergrowth. The effect of this on you will be oppressive and you will find it more difficult to energise your life.

On the other hand, if you are overlooked by electricity pylons, factories or tall chimneys, the strength of the yang influence will be overpowering, with the result that you may find your life is moving too fast for your own good.

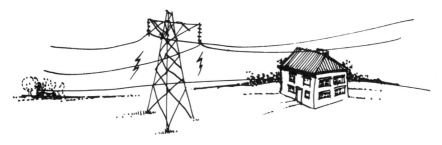

To remedy these situations, think about the symbolic qualities associated with yin and yang and introduce some of the opposing qualities to redress the existing imbalance.

To counter oppressive yin from a neighbouring building or area, first try to avoid having your main door facing the yin source, as the majority of the energy entering your home will enter through that route. If this cannot be avoided, paint the door red, a yang colour, and make sure the porch or door area is well lit; leave a light on all the time. Red is also a good colour to paint a fence or wall facing a yin direction, but other warm, bright colours will work as well. A red roof is an auspicious colour in these circumstances. If the oppressive yin is created by tall trees, cut them back if you can. If this is not possible, grow colourful flowers or flowering shrubs in front of them to introduce a balancing yang element, or think about adding a spotlight outside the house facing the yin building to illuminate and bring yang into the area.

If the problem is that the yang influence from outside is too strong, obviously your remedies will be opposite. A main door is best not positioned opposite a strong yang building or structure, but if you cannot move the door, or use another door in the house as your main door, paint it dark blue and keep it softly lit. Certainly avoid the colour red, red lights or too much brightness. Planting trees or large shrubs will add the shade of yin to the area, as will painting fences or walls in dark colours, especially blue or black, the colours of water. Water is yin, and so if you can introduce a water feature outside the house, this will also temper overactive yang; so think about creating a pond or fountain.

Yin and yang in the home

Once you have considered the overall balance in your environment, look at the rooms individually. Think about the situation as it exists, how you would like it to be, and what action will be required to perfect it. Remember that you are not necessarily looking for a middle path, an equal yin/yang balance. Usually, you will be tipping the scales slightly in favour of one energy or the other and this will relate both to the use of the room and to your personal feelings.

Don't forget that once you have made your assessment, it is a good idea to review it from time to time. You may change the decor, for example, and unintentionally shift the yin/yang balance. If you are aware of the influences, you can make sure you do this deliberately in order to activate the right kind of energy for that particular room.

Since the summer naturally has more yang energy than the winter, you could find that some areas of your home need an extra input of yang energy during the winter in order to maintain the overall harmony you have created.

Increasing the yang

When you are thinking about increasing the yang energy in a room, visualise the family living room or perhaps an office or playroom. The living room is a centre of activity, usually noisy and lively. The television and CD player are probably in the room, adding valuable yang energy, lighting may be brighter than in some other rooms in the house and perhaps there are flowers. All these elements can be used to add yang and counter oppressive yin in a room.

To bring yang energy into a room, use bright colours in your decor, especially reds and oranges. Keep curtains and soft furnishings in lighter colours, avoid too much soft drapery and pull curtains well back from the windows to allow in the maximum amount of light. Make sure the home is generally well lit, leaving lights on most of the time if necessary. Noise and activity are other aspects to consider: leave a radio playing in the background or add electrical equipment, mobiles, clocks or other moving objects to the room. You will find more about how to do this in Chapter 11 (see page 86).

Pets in the home

Pets add life – yang – to the energies in your home, so have a pet if you can. It is a great way to enliven the atmosphere. Different pets are associated with different elements, of which more in the next chapter.

Cats belong to the wood element, so it is best for their general health and well-being to choose bedding which is green or black, as green is the colour of wood and black is the colour of water, the element which supports the growth of wood. Red is not a good colour for felines as this is the colour of fire, and simple symbolism will tell you that fire and wood are not a healthy combination. For cats, the best houses are those in which the main door faces towards the east, south-east or north. People who find that stray cats gravitate towards their homes could find their doors facing in one of these directions. West and north-west are less auspicious for cats, and you could find your pet moving on to another property in which they feel the energies are more attuned to their own.

Dogs, on the other hand, belong to the element earth. Brown baskets will make them most comfortable, but you could choose red or orange. White will be inclined to act to the detriment of their health. Dogs will be happiest and healthiest living in houses in which the main door faces towards the south-west, north-east or south. If the door faces south-east or east, they will not find the energies of the house as much in their favour.

If you are unable to keep pets, ceramic or wooden ornaments or even pictures will still add a certain level of energy to the house. They even mean that you can introduce the ultimate yang 'pet' and symbol of good fortune and prosperity – the dragon – into your life.

Increasing the yin

A yin room to visualise here would be a quiet bedroom or a reading room. Lights are dim, colours are subtle and tend to be dark, activity is minimal. If you have rooms which are designed for relaxing but are too bright and overactive, think about the qualities you want to introduce in order to balance them out.

Softness and darkness are very much what is required here. Add dark, round-leaved plants or trees to the outside of the house to create shade. Use cold, muted colours, especially blue, in the decor, and steer clear of bright colours, especially red. Bright lights give too much yang; aim for a softer focus altogether, perhaps using dimmer switches or lower wattage bulbs (sometimes the remedies are that simple!). If there are too many windows, use curtains judiciously to balance the incoming light. Over-tall windows could be masked by an attractive blind at the top, or a pelmet feature. Lots of noise should be avoided. If you are making choices for pictures or ornamental features, think about images of water, or a water feature such as an aquarium.

Yin and Yang Worksheet

PERSONAL YIN/YANG QUALITIES

YIN/YANG INFLUENCES IN THE SURROUNDINGS

ACTION REQUIRED

YIN/YANG BALANCE IN THE HALL, STAIRS AND LANDING

ACTION REQUIRED

YIN/YANG BALANCE IN THE LIVING ROOM

ACTION REQUIRED

YIN/YANG BALANCE IN THE KITCHEN

ACTION REQUIRED

YIN/YANG BALANCE IN THE DINING ROOM

ACTION REQUIRED

YIN/YANG BALANCE IN THE OFFICE

ACTION REQUIRED

YIN/YANG BALANCE IN ....'S BEDROOM

ACTION REQUIRED

YIN/YANG BALANCE IN ....'S BEDROOM

ACTION REQUIRED

YIN/YANG BALANCE IN ....'S BEDROOM

ACTION REQUIRED

YIN/YANG BALANCE IN THE BATHROOM

ACTION REQUIRED

YIN/YANG BALANCE IN ....

ACTION REQUIRED

SEASONAL ADJUSTMENTS

CHAPTER 6

The Elements

All ch'i energy in the universe is a balance of yin and yang. Yin and yang evolve into the five elements: the principal energies behind the manifest physical universe.

The five basic elements are water, wood, fire, earth and metal. While in translation the word 'element' implies something of a fixed and solid nature, the Chinese word, *hsing*, in fact indicates movement and change, so a more accurate translation might be the 'five moving agents'. So we are not thinking about solid pieces of timber, for example, but the animating principles inherent in the forests.

The five elements are not static, but generate and destroy each other in a continuous cycle, as one element interacts with the next in a positive or negative way. Understanding how these divisions of ch'i energy work will enhance the potency of feng shui.

The cycle of generation

The elements are linked in a positive combination of energies, moving through a repeating cycle from water to wood to fire to earth to metal.

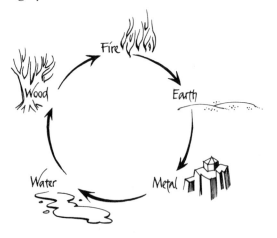

This is the cycle of generation, which is sometimes called the compatibility or positive cycle.

Water represents the biological origins of organic life. Beginning in stillness and calm, water nourishes wood. Wood grows upward and outward; its energy harnesses the growth potential which is a moving and stimulating force. Wood then nourishes fire, pulsating and vibrant, the ultimate symbol of activity. Fire burns to ashes, thus transforming into earth, where the energies are gathered together and stored. Earth hardens to form metal, a purifying and refining process. At its most pure, metal becomes liquid, classified as water, thereby renewing the cycle.

The cycle of destruction

In opposition to the cycle of generation is the incompatibility cycle, or cycle of destruction, in which the qualities of one element stand in opposition to the qualities of the next in the repeating sequence: water, fire, metal, wood, earth. This can be illustrated as a circular motion, but is easier to visualise when superimposed on the positive cycle as the second sequence creates the shape of the pentacle, the ultimate symbol of destructive power.

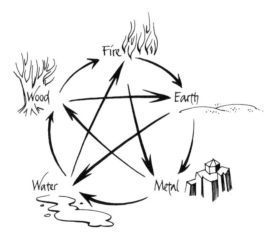

Water is able to quench fire, which melts and thus destroys metal. Metal can cut through and therefore break the life force of wood which itself drives holes in the earth, which absorbs and consumes water.

The cycle of mitigation

Looking at the same cycle, you can see that one element standing between two others can also mitigate the clash of those opposing elements. It must by now be becoming second nature to think symbolically about all such associations. Wood can soften the negative effects of water on fire by absorbing and holding back the water. Earth quenches fire and therefore softens its effect upon metal. Water nourishes wood and gives it strength to balance the influence of metal. Fire, with its power to consume wood and become earth, stands between the two. Metal mitigates between earth and water, the elements from which it is born and into which it changes.

The qualities of the elements

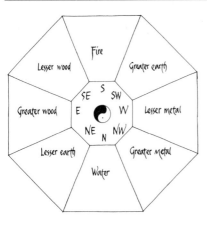

Each of the elements is associated with a particular compass direction, has a range of inherent characteristics, and is linked with particular colours and shapes. All physical things have an elemental association which can be used in a symbolic way to enhance the elemental characteristics required in a given set of circumstances. Not unusually, balance is the aim of working with elemental energies. As there are five elements and eight compass directions, the elements wood, earth and metal each relate to more than one compass zone.

The numbers associated with each element relate to the *lo shu* square (see page 114) and how that is linked with the compass directions. The animals primarily associated with each element are related to the alignment of the earthly branches (see page 119). Both these topics will be covered in more detail later.

Water

Water includes all fluids and is considered the first element, from which all others spring. Since water is a conductor of ch'i, it is linked with ch'i flow in the environment, and with roads in an urban landscape. Water is also symbolic of wealth. Associated with the north and the winter, its colours are black or blue. The shapes linked with water are undulating, like the waves or ripples on water, and it is symbolised in any water feature such as a fountain or aquarium. It is linked with the number one and with the rat and the pig.

Water has the effect of cleansing and refreshing; its purpose is renewal if used carefully, but it can be inundating if overstressed. It is associated with emotional sensitivity. Use water symbols with precision otherwise you will feel more drowned than cleansed.

Wood

The compass direction of wood is the east and to a lesser extent the south-east, its colour is green and its season is the spring. Wood shapes are long and tall, while numbers associated with the element are three and four. Any plants or flowers symbolise the wood element. Its associated animals are the tiger and the rabbit.

The characteristics of wood are strength with flexibility. It is symbolised by growth, creation and nourishment. Stimulating the areas of the home associated with wood can create positivity, although overstimulation could lead to excessive idealism.

Fire

Fire is a strong element, essentially yang in quality, alive and spirited. Not surprisingly, its associated colours are reds and oranges and its related season is the summer. It is linked with the compass direction south and with the number nine. Fire symbols include fire itself, lights and candles. Fire is particularly associated with the horse and the snake. The shapes related to fire are triangular.

Using fire symbols is a way of invigorating and stimulating areas of your life, although there is a danger of overstimulation if too much emphasis is placed on the qualities of this strong element.

Earth

Brown and yellow are the colours associated with the element earth, which belongs predominantly in the south-west but also the north-east and in the centre, the starting point for all energies. It is linked with the changing seasons: the end of the winter and the end of the summer, moving into the spring and autumn. Earth shapes are generally square, and it is associated with the numbers two, five and eight, five being the centre of the *lo shu* square. The ox, the dragon, the sheep and the dog are earth animals. Earth symbols used in feng shui are crystals and ceramics.

Earth is a supportive and reliable element, stable and confident, therefore using earth symbols can be inspiring and strengthening, while on the other hand too much earth influence can make an atmosphere stolid and over-cautious.

Metal

Metal is white, gold or silver and is linked with the north-west and also the west, with autumn and with the numbers six and seven. Circular or crescent shapes are metal shapes and any metal objects, especially gold-coloured coins, are useful symbolic objects. Metal is linked with the rooster and the monkey.

Using metal symbols encourages strength and versatility as metal is symbolised by abundance and financial success. An excess, however, can create aggression, especially in a financial sense.

Elemental shapes for buildings

As each of the elements has been described above, the shapes associated with that element have been mentioned. Undulating shapes relate to water; triangles to fire; squares to earth; rectangles and tall shapes to wood; and circles and crescents to metal.

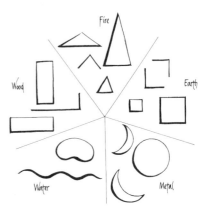

It is easy to assess your own home in relation to the basic elemental shapes simply by looking at the house. Because of their structure, most homes are earth or wood shapes. Square earth shapes offer stability and are therefore ideal. The taller wood shapes often used for office buildings denote power and success; again a good combination.

Metal shapes are circular. Strength is offered here, but also some inflexibility. This is an auspicious shape for banks and finance houses; it is not a home shape which many people will come across. Those living in lighthouses might want to counter the strength of the metal with complementary elements and the rest of the chapter will show how that can be done!

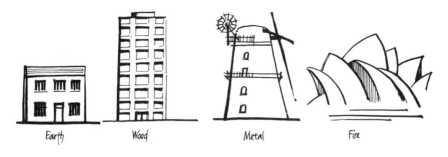

Earth   Wood   Metal   Fire

Fortunately, water shapes are unsuitable for most buildings as they are not the best elemental shapes for homes, indicating instability and flux. Fire shapes are usually too strongly yang for homes, and it is therefore appropriate that they are not often used in house construction. The passion and energy values are too great for ordinary buildings.

It is most unlikely that you have a property which features too many fire shapes, but certainly if you are building or looking to buy a property, you should avoid the Sydney Opera House! Houses which come closest to using fire shapes would be the steep-roofed chalets in mountainous districts which need the acute roof angle to prevent heavy snowfalls collecting on the roof. Although these properties may need rebalancing, the harsh, snowy environment will already demand a higher focus on the fire element, so changes may not need to be as drastic as if such a house were located in a warmer area.

The shapes of the surrounding buildings will also have an influence on your own home. You will already have considered the relative size and position of surrounding buildings in relation to the four celestial animals. In addition, fire-shaped objects or buildings around you might have given rise to *sha ch'i*, poison arrows which need to be deflected away from your property (see page 33).

Making a house plan

Discovering the qualities of the elements is not much use, however, if you cannot turn those qualities to your advantage, and to begin to do that you need to make a plan of your home. Once you have done this, you will be using it in all your feng shui calculations, so it is worth spending a little time over it if you can. For this part of the exercise, you will then be able to consider how your house relates to the qualities of the elements.

First, make a rough sketch of the area of land on which your house stands and mark in the position of the house on that plot. It can be done very accurately, but this is not essential. What you are looking to assess is the basic shape of the plot and whether the position of your house within it is harmonious.

Then make a very rough sketch of the floor plan of your house, downstairs and upstairs, marking in the positions of the doors and windows. Draw the north/south compass direction at the side of the rough plan. Then jot down on the sketch some basic room measurements. Although this takes a little time, you will find that it not only makes it easier to prepare an accurate plan, but that your rough sketch was quite likely to be inaccurate. Finally, lightly pencil the compass directions on the plan, aligning them with the north/south arrow you have drawn and centring the compass on the middle of the house so that each area is as near as possible to a similar size.

Then choose an appropriate scale to which to draw an accurate plan: for a house floor plan, one centimetre to one metre is usually workable. Later, when you prepare room plans, you can increase that scale. Using pages 57 and 58, make an accurate plan of your living space, drawing in the rooms and marking the doors and windows. Make sure you align it with the correct compass directions. If you have a garage which is integral to your property, this may influence the plan but does not count as part of your actual living space.

At this stage, it is quite adequate to make an approximate placement of the sectors relating to each of the compass directions as this chapter is concentrating on communicating an understanding of elemental principles. Because the division of the house into compass-related sectors has many other implications in feng shui, a more careful division of the home into compass zones will be dealt with later.

Plot shapes and house positions

Look first at the shape of the plot on which your home stands and the position of the house within it. A regular shape offers the best feng shui, whether it is square, rectangular, circular or semi-circular; all these are lucky as they offer the stability of earth, the growth potential of wood and the strength of metal. They also have a symmetry and regularity which is clearly good feng shui, all of which is to the advantage of those living in the house.

Irregular or sharply defined plot shapes tend to be less auspicious in feng shui terms, although this is only partly because they over-emphasise the fire element – however important passion and activity are to life, they are not the most stable emotions on which to build. This is also because irregular plots tend to lack balance and symmetry – the basic aim of feng shui – and also because they can create shapes which encourage poor circulation of ch'i: sharp corners, acute angles and wasted spaces. If your house is on a plot which is triangular or very

irregular, it will be beneficial to take some steps to achieve a more balanced shape.

You can do this by erecting fences or planting trees or shrubs to block off sharp-angled corners and encourage a more regular aspect to the shape of the plot. It is best if the main door of the house does not face directly towards a sharp corner of the plot. If this is the case, a fence or shrubs can be positioned to block off the corner, or you could consider using another door or adding a porch. These actions will also have the effect of negating any *sha ch'i*.

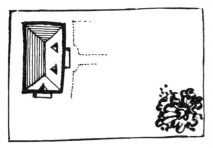

The ideal position for the house is roughly within the central one-third of the plot, again establishing the principle of balance. If this is not the case, it may be worth considering ways of re-establishing a symmetry within the plot. For example, if the house is placed at the end of a long plot, plant a tree or place a large statue in the opposite corner. Lighting up one area of the house will also serve to give it more prominence and encourage balance.

The shape of the floor plan

As with the shape of the plot, the shape of the floor plan is also important. Home floor-plan shapes are usually square earth or rectangular wood shapes, which is good feng shui. Again, the lighthouse-keeper may wish to strengthen complementary elements to balance the metal shape of the house. If the overall floor plan is an irregular one, however, often owing to the house having been extended or altered since it was originally built, this is not ideal feng shui. However, because this has more implications than just those associated with the elements, we will be looking at ways of redressing this balance in more detail later. At this stage, the application of the qualities of the elements is the most important consideration.

Balancing the elements

From the plan you have drawn, you can see which areas of your home relate to each of the five elements. As you might expect, the aim is to have a balance of all five. If you have a perfectly regular floor plan, this may already be the case. But most people will be able to see an imbalance in favour of one or more of the elements. This can create a comparable imbalance in their lives. For example, if a house has too strong an emphasis on the fire element, the occupants may find that they are prone to be positive and active to the point of being argumentative or even aggressive. If earth is too dominant, they may be stable and sensible to the exclusion of all other emotions.

The elemental cycles of generation, destruction and mitigation are the key to restoring balance. You can use symbols of each of the elements to influence the qualities of your home and the direction of your life, placing them in the area of the home in which they will be most effective. Add more of one element, or strengthen or soften those characteristics by adding others. The circumstances have to be extreme for you to consider adding an opposing element, as this is generally not good feng shui.

Using colour and symbols

One of the simplest ways of affecting the elemental qualities is with the use of colour. All the descriptions on pages 46–48 have linked individual

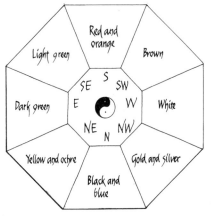

elements with specific colours: water is associated with blue or black; wood with green; fire with red and orange; earth with brown and yellow; metal with white, gold and silver. Relating these colours to the elemental cycles can help you to strengthen or mitigate the effects of any of the elements in your home.

Symbolic objects can be used in the same way. Actual objects made from the element are obviously a good choice: an aquarium, wooden, ceramic or metal objects and so on. You can also choose representations of the elements: photographs or pictures of landscapes or water, for example.

Remember too that shapes are related to the elements, so you can also use shapes to encourage elemental qualities. A rectangular wooden table has two wood qualities, making it a stronger symbol than a round wooden one.

Elemental qualities in individual rooms

In the same way that the southern area of the house relates to the fire element, so the southern area of each room also relates to that element, the north to water and so on. You can apply the same principles to using the elements in individual rooms as you can to using them in the home. Consider this in more detail when you come to assess the individual rooms of your home.

Your personal element

According to your year of birth, you will be associated on a personal level with one of the five elements. This may affect your natural instincts and the way you interact with the other elements in terms of the need for particular qualities in the home and in individual rooms, the use of colour and so on. This will be looked at in more detail later in the book (see page 99).

Using the qualities of the elements

Go through the zones of your house and assess whether the elements in that sector are harmonious. Try to achieve overall harmony throughout the building for the most positive benefits.

The north – water

In the northern part of the house, water colours and symbols are sympathetic, but avoid drowning the area with too much black and blue. If your family is already over-emotional, you may be better to add green and wood to temper that direction. Supportive and strengthening colours would be the gold, silver or white of metal; in fact the additional strength which they symbolise may well be more beneficial to the overall balance of energies you want to create than adding more water symbols. Earth colours are generally not at home as they will have a smothering effect.

The east and south-east – wood

Greens are appropriate in the east and south-east if you want to emphasise the growth potential of wood. Supportive colours are the black and blue of water, which will add some more emotional and intuitive qualities. As in all sectors, an overall balance is the aim, so don't overdo one element, especially in its allocated zone. Negative colours are the white, gold and silver of metal, while reds will temper an over-strong wood influence.

The south – fire

The south relates to the element fire and therefore to reds and oranges, but avoid over-using these colours in the southern sector, otherwise the power of the element can become aggressive rather than passionate. Use green and wooden objects or symbols to support fire and direct its energies correctly. Blue and black will drown the element completely. Brown and yellow may be a very useful addition and stabilise what can be a volatile zone.

The south-west and north-east – earth

The south-west and north-east relate to the earth element and therefore suitable colours are brown and yellow ochre. A stable and sensible family may not need this additional earth stimulation, however, but may find the addition of some passionate fire colours or symbols more beneficial. Metal will lessen the effects of earth – useful if the family is in a boring rut, for example – while the qualities of wood will have a strongly negative effect.

The north-west and west – metal

The north-west and west relate to the element metal, so the colours which are sympathetic in these sectors are gold or silver and white, while the symbolism is of metal objects. If you want to enhance the strong qualities of metal in that area, you can emphasise those colours. To provide support and stability to underpin that strength, introduce earth colours of brown and yellow. Take care not to use red or the symbolism of fire unless you are bent on destroying the metal element. To mellow the effects of its strength and add more intuitive qualities, you would be better to add blue or black.

Reference guide to using the qualities of the elements

Water

Water relates to emotional sensitivity.
Water colours: blue and black.
Water shapes: uneven or undulating.
Water symbols and images: mirrors; glass; water features such as a fish tank or fountain; images of waterfalls, seascapes and fish.

Use the cycle of generation to support	Add water or metal
Use the cycle of destruction to reduce	Add earth
Use the cycle of mitigation to soften	Add wood

Wood

Wood inspires creativity, growth and nourishment.
Wood colours: greens.
Wood shapes: rectangular, tall and thin.

Wood symbols and images: wooden objects; plants; cane or wicker furniture; rush mats; images of trees and plants.

Use the cycle of generation to support	Add wood or water
Use the cycle of destruction to reduce	Add metal
Use the cycle of mitigation to soften	Add fire

Fire

Fire relates to motivation, action, passion and intellect.

Fire colours: reds and oranges.

Fire shapes: triangular.

Fire symbols and images: animal-based materials; candles; lights; images of light or fire, sunsets and sunrises.

Use the cycle of generation to support	Add fire or wood
Use the cycle of destruction to reduce	Add water
Use the cycle of mitigation to soften	Add earth

Earth

Earth inspires stability, confidence and reliability.

Earth colours: browns and yellows.

Earth shapes: square.

Earth symbols and images: ceramic; stone objects; crystals; images of landscapes.

Use the cycle of generation to support	Add earth or fire
Use the cycle of destruction to reduce	Add wood
Use the cycle of mitigation to soften	Add metal

Metal

Metal offers strength, abundance and financial success.

Metal colours: white, gold and silver.

Metal shapes: round, dome- or crescent-shapes.

Metal symbols and images: metal objects; swords; images of coins or metal.

Use the cycle of generation to support	Add metal or earth
Use the cycle of destruction to reduce	Add fire
Use the cycle of mitigation to soften	Add water

Elements Worksheet

....

ELEMENTAL HOUSE SHAPE

....

ACTION REQUIRED

....

ELEMENTAL SHAPES OF NEIGHBOURING PROPERTIES

....

ACTION REQUIRED

....

Plot Shape and House Position

....

ACTION REQUIRED

....

....

....

....

....

....

....

Floor plan downstairs

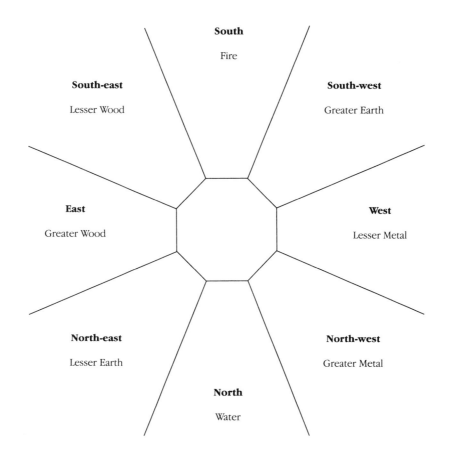

ACTION IN WATER SECTOR

ACTION IN WOOD SECTORS

ACTION IN FIRE SECTOR

ACTION IN EARTH SECTORS

ACTION IN METAL SECTORS

Floor plan upstairs

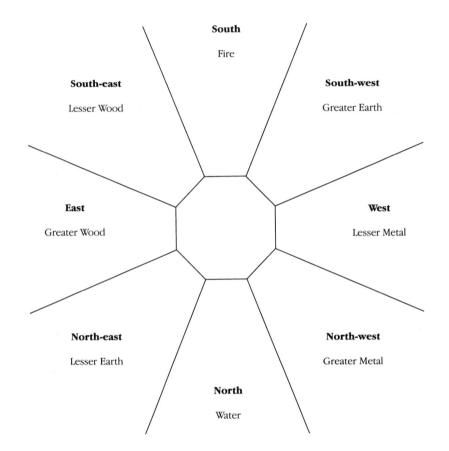

South

Fire

South-east

Lesser Wood

South-west

Greater Earth

East

Greater Wood

West

Lesser Metal

North-east

Lesser Earth

North-west

Greater Metal

North

Water

ACTION IN WATER SECTOR

ACTION IN WOOD SECTORS

ACTION IN FIRE SECTOR

ACTION IN EARTH SECTORS

ACTION IN METAL SECTORS

CHAPTER 7

The Trigrams

The universe is a balance of yin and yang. The balance between the two creates different types of energy, thus a predominantly yang energy will be different in quality from a predominantly yin energy. These qualities evolve into the five elements which are linked with specific compass directions and with eight divisions of ch'i energy. Each of these divisions is represented by a Chinese name and a trigram – a group of three lines which illustrates its yin/yang balance. Each one is also linked with a special member of the family and has a range of inherent characteristics.

It is essential to understand the characteristics of the energy associated with the eight basic trigrams when beginning to apply feng shui to your home. Their qualities can then be used carefully to best advantage. This chapter examines the trigrams and their associations so that in the next, all the various aspects of the topic can be brought together.

Ch'ien

Ch'ien is the yang trigram which relates to the father or the male head of the household and to all men over the age of forty-six. Its symbol is heaven and it is related to the greater metal element, indicating strength and immobility. Associated colours are therefore gold and silver. The changing season from autumn to winter is indicated by this sector, which is positioned in the north-west.

K'an

K'an

K'an is associated with the middle son of the household and men between sixteen and thirty. It relates to the element water and therefore the colours black and blue and the season of winter, which is aligned with the northerly direction. Its symbol is also water. Qualities of this sector's energy involve movement and change.

Ken

Ken

Symbolised by a mountain, *ken* relates to the youngest son in the household, boys up to the age of fifteen and the direction north-east. Lesser earth is the relevant element here and the colour yellow. This segment relates to changing seasons, winter moving to spring. Motivation, purpose and knowledge are the strongest energies.

Chen

Chen

Positioned in the east, *chen* is the trigram of the eldest son of the household and men between thirty-one and forty-five. Dark green is the colour of the greater wood element here, the season is spring and the symbol thunder. This is an outward-moving energy relating to decision-making and ambition.

Hsun

Hsun

Related to the eldest daughter and women from thirty-one to forty-five, the *hsun* trigram is in the south-east. Lighter green and lesser wood are its colour and element. The symbol of *hsun* is the wind. Expanding energies here relate to wealth and the south-east is often known as the fortunate blessings direction.

Li

Li

In the south, the season is summer, symbolised by the sun or by lightning. Red is the colour of this sector, which is linked with the middle daughter or women from sixteen to thirty. An upward-moving energy resides here, encouraging passion and recognition.

K'un

The yin symbol of *k'un* relates to the mother of the house and women over the age of forty-six. In the south-west, it is an earth symbol with the colour brown, associated with late summer. Greater earth is also the symbol of this sector. All the qualities of the maternal apply: strong relationships, caring and enveloping energies, trust and understanding.

Tui

Moving to the western sector, *tui* represents the youngest daughter and girls up to the age of fifteen. The symbol of this direction is a lake, and it relates to the element lesser metal and the colour white. Relationships are again a feature of the energy here, related to children, creativity, joy and romance.

The trigrams reference sheet

Ch'ien		father	NW	heaven	late autumn	greater metal	gold & silver
K'an		middle son	N	water	winter	water	black dark-blue
Ken		youngest son	NE	mountain	late winter	lesser earth	ochre
Chen		eldest son	E	thunder	spring	greater wood	dark green
Hsun		eldest daughter	SE	wind	early summer	lesser wood	light green
Li		middle daughter	S	sun/ lightning	summer	fire	red
K'un		mother	SW	earth	late summer	greater earth	brown
Tui		youngest daughter	W	lake	autumn	lesser metal	white

CHAPTER 8

The Bagua

It has already become clear that the elements of feng shui are linked together and begin to overlap and interconnect in a variety of different ways. The linking symbol is the bagua, or pa kua, which simply means 'grid'. Based on the compass, the trigrams are positioned around the compass points, thus creating a position for the various qualities associated with them. By using the bagua on the arrangement of rooms in your home, and on individual rooms, you can optimise the energies within the family.

The earlier heaven sequence

The original arrangement of the trigrams around the compass is known as the earlier heaven sequence. The positions of the trigrams represent the ancient or heavenly order and are used only in the feng shui of tombs and finding the optimum position for grave sites.

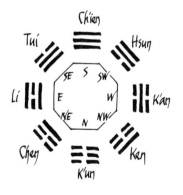

Ch'ien, the yang trigram, is positioned in the south opposite *k'un*, the yin trigram in the north, as these are opposites. Similarly, *li* in the east is opposite *k'an* in the west; *tui* in the south-east opposes *ken* in the north-west; and *hsun* in the south-west is opposite to *chen* in the north-east. Thus the arrangement illustrates the perfect symmetry of the ideal, with symbolic opposites balancing each other on the grid: the universal opposites of heaven and earth; the organic opposites of fire and water; the elemental opposites of mountain and lake; and the impulsive opposites of wind and thunder.

The later heaven sequence

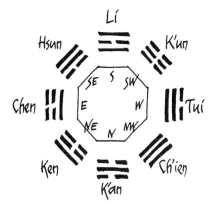

As in life itself, the arrangement which is appropriate for the homes of the living does not illustrate this perfect symmetry. It is the later heaven sequence which is used in all feng shui relating to homes and offices and which is therefore appropriate to this book.

The application of the bagua to your living areas is simple and versatile. Because of the qualities and relationships which are best served by each of the compass directions, you can apply the bagua to your home, your office or an individual room by overlaying the bagua on to a plan of the area, relating it to ordinary compass directions. This will show you which areas of the home are most suited to particular activities and for particular members of the household.

The divisions of ch'i energy

We have already looked at the basic principles relating to each of the trigrams and seen that they also relate to one particular member of the family or age range of men or women.

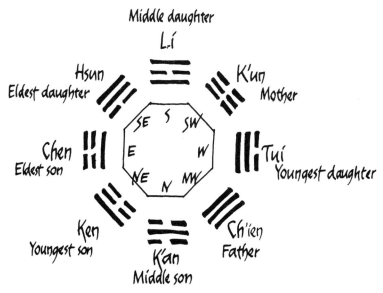

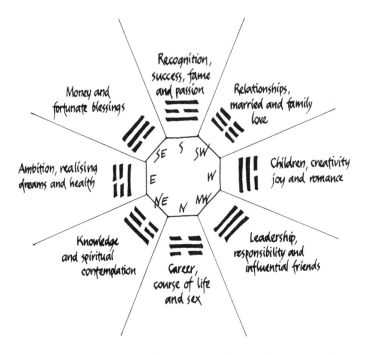

The ch'i energy in each sector has particular qualities which make it appropriate for certain of life's activities. Applying this in detail to the bagua arrangement and relating it to your home means that you can access the various qualities of the ch'i energy.

The north-west

The north-west, *ch'ien*, relates to the father of the household and to men over forty-six. The support of influential people is the most important aspect of luck in this sector.

The main qualities of the ch'i in this zone relate to responsibility, planning and leadership. It is an inward-moving energy creating its own strength and purpose and fostering the characteristics of leadership and organisation. The north-western part of the house is therefore a good place to position the office or bedroom of the main breadwinner of the house, or for those who have reached a stable position in their career.

The north

The independent middle son or men between sixteen and thirty relate to the northern sector, *k'an*. Water represents the journey of life and is linked to career and the choices you make in relation to how you structure your life's path. It generally has a meandering and stable energy which relates to independence or even solitude.

Tap into that quiet, tranquil energy by using the northern part of the house as the main bedroom, to encourage a stable sex life and a contented relationship, or as the bedroom or main room for the young men in the house. It is also a good position for meditation so a room which is used for quiet contemplation would be well positioned here. Having considered deeply the course your life is taking, northern energies are also good for activating changes to improve your situation.

The north-east

Boys up to the age of fifteen, the youngest sons, are most relevant to the north-eastern sector, *ken*. The search for knowledge is characterised by this area of the house with its strong, sharp and direct energy, quick to change and eager to get its own way. Knowledge of self is also represented here, so it can also be used to tap into energies associated with spiritual contemplation.

This is the best area of the house for learning and education; position the bedrooms of the youngest male members of the house here. Students and those wanting to clarify their aims in life will find this a good zone. The energies support decision-making and give drive to attain desired goals. Since the energies are also associated with physical drive, it is also an appropriate place for playrooms.

The east

The eastern sector, *chen*, relates to the eldest son and men between thirty-one and forty-five. Health is an important aspect of the ch'i energy in this sector, as is developing ambition and realising dreams. The energy is forward-looking and optimistic, an active and focused ch'i surrounding the ambition of the eldest son.

Place the studies of the male members of the family in the east, or use it for the kitchen or a hobby room which will benefit from the active and practical energies.

The south-east

Hsun is the sector of the eldest daughter and women from thirty-one to forty-five. Wealth and prosperity are the most important factors in the south-east. Again the energy is active, but less aggressive than in the east and more suited to a mature progress.

Place the kitchen in the south-east sector, or use the sector for the bedroom or study of female members of the family as it will help them to make the most of their natural talents.

The south

The middle daughter relates to the southern sector, *li*, as well as women from sixteen to thirty years old. A passionate energy resides here and relates to respect, recognition and fame.

The south is a good position for the dining room if it is used for entertaining, or for an office room. As it is a strong and passionate energy, it is suitable for a bedroom if the occupants are in need of some stimulation for their sex life, but is not as suitable for those who want sleep and relaxation.

The south-west

K'un is the sector relating to the mother of the house and women over forty-six. Love and happy marital relationships are the important factor here. The tranquil energy encourages strong relationships and emotional security, as well as promoting practicality in problem-solving.

This is the best place to position the living or family dining room. It is also excellent for the bedroom as it will encourage a trusting and loving relationship.

The west

The youngest daughter of the house and girls up to the age of fifteen relate to the western sector, *tui*. It is the sector of the house which is particularly associated with children, creativity, joy and romance.

It is good for a dining or living room for a family with children and will encourage a deep and loving family structure. Both children and adolescents with their bedrooms in the west will feel loved and safe.

The centre

The centre of the bagua is important for all the family as it is the source of all the energies in the house. It is related to the earth and the colours yellow and brown and to the spiritual, emotional and physical health of the family. The centre of the house should be kept clear and uncluttered to allow the free movement of the ch'i energy through the house. It is a good place to position the main family living room or anywhere where all the members of the family congregate and there is laughter and interaction. If the heart of the home tends to be silent – perhaps it is a store room or unused room – or if it suffers from *sha ch'i* – a toilet is sited in the centre, for example – this will adversely affect the feng shui of the entire home.

Activating the energies in your home

You have already made a plan of your home and looked at it in relation to the elements. In an extension of that process, it is now time to look at the plan in relation to the qualities of the ch'i energy in each of the compass sectors.

In the first place, the question of balance must be addressed as many people will not have the perfectly regular floor plan which makes ideal feng shui. The house may have been extended and have an additional area jutting out from the main body of the house, or it may have an indent, with part of one or more of the zones missing. Before you can accurately apply the bagua to your home, you need to take steps to eliminate these imbalances.

Property extensions

Many modern houses have been extended and this means that your floor plan may be irregular. This is not ideal feng shui and will have an effect on the nature of the energy in the home because it will cause an imbalance between the different sectors. If your house has an extension, measure on your plan its width along the adjoining wall. Then measure the length the building extends from that wall. An extension which is less than half as long as the width of the adjoining wall will have a positive effect on the area of the house in which it falls, so no action needs to be taken. Extensions which are larger than this will cause the ch'i to be unbalanced and the corresponding elemental qualities of that portion will be exaggerated.

Because the qualities of the ch'i energies in each sector relate to individuals, they may influence one member of the family more than another. Because the energies are associated with the elements, those qualities are also relevant and are used to redress any imbalances. This work is therefore complementary to considerations you made in the chapter on the elements.

Extensions in the north-west and west

Small extensions in the north-west and west are good for the overall strength of the occupants as they relate to the element metal. They should encourage a steady build-up of career prospects and advantages gained through influential contacts. In the west, a small extension will be to the advantage of the children, while anyone with a creative flair will find it easier to develop their talents. In the north-west, the benefit will primarily be reaped by the older men in the family and those in positions of responsibility.

Extensions which over-emphasise the metal element in these areas, however, can cause members of the family to become intractable and lose the ability to compromise, perhaps even becoming unable to deal with emotional issues. If the 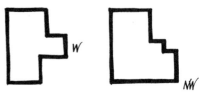 extension is in the north-west, the husband or father may well become too arrogant and domineering. In the western sector, the children could lean towards extreme wilfulness. Issues of poor health relate to the large intestines or lungs and general good fortune will decline.

The remedy is to activate the water element in the extension in order to reduce the effect of the overabundance of metal. Use black or dark blue in the decor or in ornaments or paintings. You could also hang a blue-framed or black-framed mirror on the west- or north-west-facing wall. Yellows and browns will support the metal still further, so avoid these colours, ceramic objects and any earth symbols as well as metal colours or objects.

Extensions in the south-west and north-east

Small extensions in the north-east encourage good motivation and will be especially good for students. In the south-west, a small extended area will give support to the cohesion of the family and good marital and family relationships.

Where the earth element is over-emphasised in these areas by a large extension, however, this can lead to selfishness and greed. Family members may become inward-looking and eventually lose motivation and financial advantage by being too grasping. If the 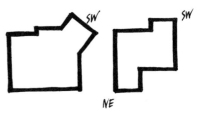 extension is in the south-west, the mother may be over-dominant. Health issues will be likely to relate to eating disorders.

Use white to modify the excessive effects of earth in these areas. Mirrors with gold or silver frames can be hung on the south-west- or north-east-facing walls. Generally, stimulate the metal element to recreate a more even balance. Keep away from earth colours and symbols and remember that fire energy will serve to support earth, so also avoid red colours, candles or other fire symbols.

Extensions in the south

In the south, small extensions will encourage a sociable outlook, a good circle of friends and perhaps even public recognition.

Excess of passion will be encouraged by overstimulation of this fire area: volatile emotions, stress and tension of all kinds. High blood pressure and heart disorders are the likely health problems which may be encountered.

Calm the passion of fire with earth symbols. Use yellow or brown colours in the decor and hang a mirror on the south-facing wall to deflect the energies. Avoid using too much wood, which would feed the fire, but choose ceramics and earth symbols to stimulate the earth element. Reds and oranges are also best left out of the extension.

Extensions in the south-east and east

Harmonious relationships and financial good fortune are associated with small extensions in the south-east, while those with the eastern area gently stimulated by a small addition to the house may find their dreams coming to realisation. The south-east will particularly benefit the eldest daughter and the east the eldest son.

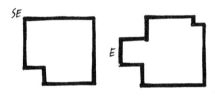

Larger structures creating an imbalance in the wood element will tend to make the occupants try too hard to succeed, creating anger and disappointment. Their forward vision may not be clear, their ambitions impossible to realise. If the exension is in the south-east, financial problems could result. Ill-health is likely to relate to the liver or other organs.

Fire will burn off the excessive strength of the wood element, so use reds and oranges, and hang a mirror on the south-east- or east-facing wall, preferably with a red frame. Blue is the colour to avoid as are water symbols which will strengthen and support the wood still further, and clearly you will not need more green colours in this zone.

Extensions in the north

In the northern sector, small extensions will encourage independence and a steady advancement along the career path.

If the water element is thrown out of balance by a large extension in the north, however, you may experience a feeling of being overwhelmed,

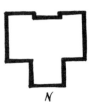

drowned by problems and difficulties. Difficulties in your career will cause stress and encourage depression. Occupants may find that they have problems with nervous conditions, joint or kidney problems. There may be a tendency to try to withdraw from the problems of life, leading to isolation.

N

Activate wood to absorb the water. Use plants, especially water-loving plants such as reeds, to decorate the extension. Green colours will be beneficial as well as wooden furniture or ornaments. Try to avoid adding more blue or black, and keep away from white, silver and gold, the metal colours or symbols which would enhance the wood qualities.

Missing sections of a property

In a similar way, if the shape of the house shows an indented section, or an extension creates an overall shape in which a particular section is missing altogether, this situation will need to be rectified. Chinese houses built on feng shui principles would not be constructed around a central courtyard as this would mean that the centre of the bagua was missing, affecting the cohesion of the whole family.

Whether an extension is creating an imbalance or a section is missing, the aim is to recreate a regular shape, either actually or symbolically, thereby giving each sector its proper balance overall, and to avoid overstimulation or depression of one of the main energies.

If you can re-establish a regular shape by building an extension to regularise the shape of the house, obviously this is ideal, but in most cases this is, of course, not possible. If you are considering building a

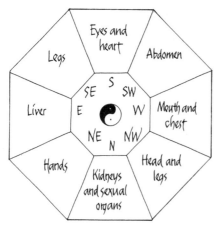

conservatory or other addition to the house, however, it is worth thinking about using this opportunity to restore the balance, and certainly not to create problems which do not already exist. There are, however, other ways to replace the missing parts symbolically.

Since the energy directions are also associated with parts of the body, missing sections of the house can relate to illnesses or health problems in those physical areas.

Sections missing in the north-west and west

If the north-western or western zones are missing, then metal is out of balance. Weakness of character may result, as well as a breakdown of communicaton. The north-west will particularly affect the fortunes of the father or the major breadwinner in the family. The west may have

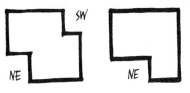

more effect on the children and make them feel unstable and possibly unloved. Respiration or elimination problems become more likely.

If you paint the walls around the extended area white or place mirrors on the north-west- or north-facing walls, this will give the illusion of a complete area. Use round metal shapes for the mirrors and other furniture if possible.

Sections missing in the south-west and north-east

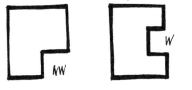

When earth is depressed, this is likely to result in feelings of insecurity, as if the ground is not steady beneath you. A weakness in the mother could be particularly evident if the south-west is missing, as could a general disharmony in either marital or general family relationships. Missing a north-eastern sector is more likely to have a detrimental effect on the young people in the house, especially students. Disturbed sleep and poor nourishment are symptomatic of missing earth zones.

Paint the walls around the missing sections in yellows or browns and use square-shaped furniture or mirrors on the walls, preferably with brown or yellow frames. Avoid the use of reds or oranges.

Sections missing in the south

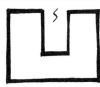

Being without the southern section of the house means that the social life will be less than it should be, and occupants will be inclined to emotional coldness and find difficulty relating to other people. Poor eyesight and circulation can be indicated.

South-facing walls are best painted in fairly strong fire colours, or use rugs or small ornaments in reds and oranges or even purple. Pictures should be chosen with the support of the fire element in mind.

Sections missing in the south-east and east

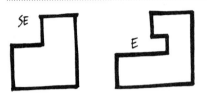

Zones of the house missing from the south-eastern portion are not good for the financial prospects of those living in the house, while a missing eastern section will adversely affect the health of the family, particularly in general debility or liver problems. The depression of the wood element can mean confusion and an inability to look forward and outward as the expanding energies of these sectors are missing.

Bolster the wood element with green colours, well-tended plants and mirrors with green frames on the south-east- or east-facing walls. Blue in small quantities can give additional support.

Sections missing in the north

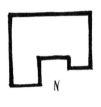

Losing the northern section of the house affects mainly the men, and their career prospects in particular. Occupants may be unable to think clearly and adapt to situations which arise in their lives. Sexual problems are the most likely health risk along with illnesses affecting the kidneys or poor elimination.

Blue walls will help to activate the missing water energies, with a mirror on the north-facing wall; choose a black frame if possible. A water feature, such as a small aquarium, could be placed against the wall.

Using the outside space

In all cases, it is also possible to use the outside of the house so that the missing corner is activated and brought back into relevance. This can be done in addition to measures taken inside the house. One way is to install a light in the missing corner of the plot, as this will serve to energise the elemental qualities outside the house. Another way is to landscape the area with plants and garden furniture so that in effect, it becomes an outside room, but do not use this option if you already have an excess of wood energies in the home. Both of these methods help to restore life to the part of the house which was 'missing' from the regular plan.

Activating your plan

Go back to your floor plans or drawn them out again. Centre the bagua over the plan so that the compass sectors are as evenly balanced as possible and the centre is positioned over the heart of the home. Align the bagua correctly with the compass directions. Think about how you are going to rebalance the elements, activate any missing sections and reduce dominant qualities in extensions or awkward shapes. Then think about the existing uses of the rooms and consider whether they are ideal in relation to the feng shui information you have learned. Concentrate on the activity which is most often undertaken in that room. If the allocation is not ideal, can the use of the rooms be changed? This is sometimes possible, particularly with the allocation of bedrooms. For example, if the bedroom in the west is used by a young man who is just starting university, while his younger brother has his room in the north-east, it might be advantageous to both of them to exchange rooms.

Clearly for many people, the position of rooms will be fixed, especially for kitchens and living rooms in most houses. In that case, you need to consider how to make the best use of the energies available in the rooms. To do this, you simply apply the bagua to the room itself rather than to the overall floor plan; you can then stimulate the particular sections of the room most suited to the use of the room itself. This will be examined later in the book.

The Bagua Worksheet

Floor plan downstairs

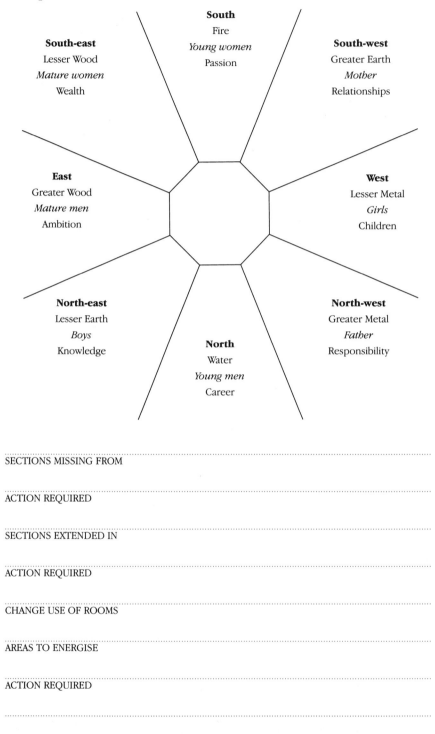

South
Fire
Young women
Passion

South-east
Lesser Wood
Mature women
Wealth

South-west
Greater Earth
Mother
Relationships

East
Greater Wood
Mature men
Ambition

West
Lesser Metal
Girls
Children

North-east
Lesser Earth
Boys
Knowledge

North
Water
Young men
Career

North-west
Greater Metal
Father
Responsibility

SECTIONS MISSING FROM

ACTION REQUIRED

SECTIONS EXTENDED IN

ACTION REQUIRED

CHANGE USE OF ROOMS

AREAS TO ENERGISE

ACTION REQUIRED

The Bagua Worksheet

Floor plan upstairs

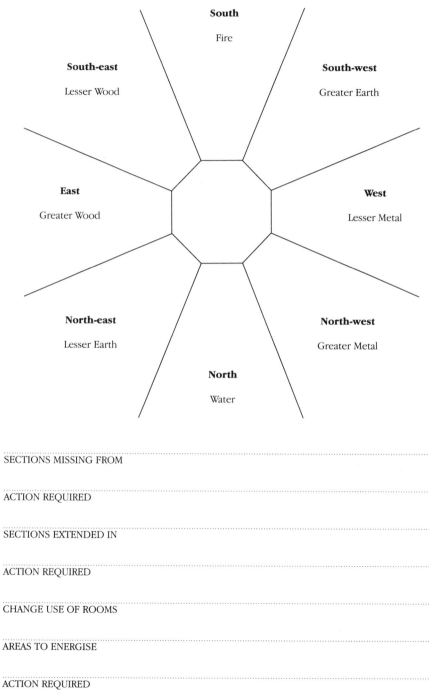

SECTIONS MISSING FROM

ACTION REQUIRED

SECTIONS EXTENDED IN

ACTION REQUIRED

CHANGE USE OF ROOMS

AREAS TO ENERGISE

ACTION REQUIRED

CHAPTER 9

The Main Door
of your Home

When we looked at the flow of ch'i energies around and into the
home, it became clear that the main door of the house is crucial
to the flow of ch'i into the house. Ch'i circulates in the surrounding area
and, in ideal circumstances, is allowed to settle and accumulate in the
space in front of the house. The main flow of ch'i into the house is then
through the front door because the ch'i flow is encouraged by the
movement of people in and out of the house. The door is sometimes
called the *kou*, or the mouth of the home, into which all auspicious and
inauspicious ch'i makes its way.

Checking the main door

It is therefore important to ensure first that the door is not confronted
by killing arrows, and this has already been dealt with in earlier
chapters. Stand at the front door and look out. Check again that there
are no sharp corners or eaves, satellite dishes, lamp posts or spires
directing *sha ch'i* into your front door. If there are any you have missed
in your previous examinations, deal with them now (see page 33).

Ideally, there should be a space outside the main door and a small rise
in front, as you will remember from the discussion of form-school feng
shui and the celestial animals. Hedges, fences and shrubs are the best
way to supply any deficiency (see pages 24–5). A water feature at the
front – perhaps a bird bath or a fountain – will create auspicious
circumstances.

Obstructions in front of the main door are not good feng shui. If there
is no space in front of the door for the ch'i to accumulate, it is a good
idea to energise the area by using a colour appropriate to the direction
in which the door is facing and to make sure that the area is constantly
well lit.

If the main door is at the foot of a flight of stairs, this can encourage
poor health among members of the family. A simple way to avoid this is

to raise the threshold by one or two centimetres so that you have to step over the threshold into the house. The same remedy can be used if the door is facing a lift, which confuses the flow of ch'i.

If a main door is at the top of a flight of steps, the occupants may find that they cannot hold on to money. A mirror placed outside the house to reflect the negative energies can be helpful. This is also a good remedy to apply if the door is opposite to a lift.

The direction of the main door

The sector of the house in which the main door falls as well as the direction in which it faces should be considered in relation to the head of the family. In traditional Chinese families in the past, this was always the eldest male in the household. Nowadays, of course, this decision is no longer straightforward and you will have to consider how the direction relates to the needs of both yourself and your partner. It is possible to compromise so that the optimum direction for both of you is obtained. You need to consider both your place in the family and also your personal auspicious directions, which are calculated later in the book (see page 103).

If you are looking at a new property, try to choose one which is aligned in the best possible direction for the main breadwinner, or as a compromise between the main members of the household. If you are already in a property, consider the implications of the direction of the main door and take positive action, if necessary, to improve the feng shui prospects.

If the door is facing the north-west, this is a good direction for fathers and older men. It will encourage sound qualities of leadership and dignity in that member of the family, who will earn the trust and respect of the other occupants.

A door facing towards the north can encourage a quiet life for the occupants, although there is a possibility that things can become too quiet and that those living there may even become isolated. This is a case in which the qualities of the opposing element can be introduced to energise different characteristics. Add a little earth to the water to reduce the strength of the energies by painting the door brown or yellow and hanging a crystal inside the doorway.

The north-east can be a problematic direction, since the energies can be changeable and the occupants can find that they become susceptible to outside influences, although if other feng shui indicators are auspicious, it can be a good direction for young people wanting to expand their knowledge and education.

East-facing doors are good for the young, particularly if they are embarking on a new career. The auspices are good for those who wish to realise their dreams and ambitions, and indicate a bright future for those in business or commercial operations.

A door facing towards the south-east will benefit from less aggressive energies than an east-facing door, but it is nonetheless a good direction for the young in particular, and for those seeking to improve their financial situation. Progress will be slow but sure, and the occupants should enjoy good social connections and lives which are both harmonious and creative.

South-facing doors encourage an active and sociable life, with the occupants looking outward for recognition and even fame. It is worth taking care, however, that these energies do not become too strong, creating an over-stressed atmosphere. Tempering the fire with water may even become necessary.

If you are living in a house where the door faces south-west, this will benefit the mother of the house. Strong and loving marital relationships are encouraged here, although there can be a danger that the mother can become too dominant and overbearing, in which case the overall feeling will be one of becoming stuck in a rut. If this is the case, introduce some wood colours or symbols to temper that effect, or energise the elements with fire symbols.

West-facing doors are good for families with young children and will provide the best opportunities for their happy and creative development. Romance and pleasure will be well represented, but be careful that the relaxed nature of the energies does not encourage overspending. A little of the stability of earth could be used to advantage here.

Elemental colours and shapes

You have already established the direction in which the main door of your house is facing. By choosing appropriate colours based on the direction the door faces, you can support or energise different elements. For example, if you want to energise the qualities of stability in a south-west facing door, then you can paint it red, whereas if the occupants of the house are more in need of a secure foundation in their lives, they should choose brown or yellow. If circumstances change, then the colour of the door is easily altered. Always refer to the cycle of generation (see page 44).

If the door is facing north-west or west, white, gold or silver will energise the facing metal element, while brown or yellow will be supportive. Avoid red, blue or black. North-facing doors can be painted in blue or black, or in supportive white. Avoid brown and yellow or green. If the door is facing north-east or south-west, use brown or yellow, or supportive red or orange. Avoid green and white. Doors facing east or south-east can best use green, black or blue but not white. South-facing doors can use red or green, but are best not painted in blue or black or, to a lesser extent, brown or yellow.

As well as using elemental colours, you can use the shapes related to the elements to enhance the qualities of ch'i coming in through your main door. Think about the cycle of generation of the elements and use shapes to energise or support the element related to the direction in which the door faces (see page 48).

Use water shapes to energise the cleansing qualities of water for doors facing north; or metal shapes for strength and support. Use wood shapes to energise possibilities for growth for doors facing east or south-east; or water shapes for cleansing and renewal. Use fire shapes to invigorate the occupants of houses with doors facing south; or wood shapes for growth. Use earth shapes to emphasise stability for doors facing south-west or north-east; or fire shapes to invigorate and enliven.

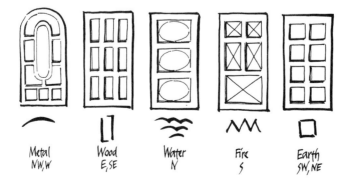

Metal
NW, W

Wood
E, SE

Water
N

Fire
S

Earth
SW, NE

Use metal shapes to give strength for doors facing west or north-west;
or earth shapes for stability.

Door styles

The best style for a door is solid and protective rather than glass. Ideally,
the main door should be the largest door in the house to encourage the
best ch'i flow into the building and it should be larger than the largest
occupant of the house, so that everyone can move freely into the house
without cramping their aura. It is best if the door opens into the house.
If it opens outwards, it makes better feng shui sense to alter the hinges.

If there are windows on either side of the door, it is possible that the
ch'i will flow in through the door and straight out through the windows.
Shield them with net curtains or place a green plant in front of each
window. The plants will also encourage good fortune in the home.

Where the door opens

It is best if there is a space on to which the main door opens, so that the
ch'i entering the house is calmed and settled before it begins to move
through the house. If the space is cramped, add mirrors and light to
uplift the ch'i energies.

A main door directly opposite the back door can create a rush of ch'i
into and straight out of the house. Use a crystal or a wind chime to slow
the flow of ch'i and prevent it rushing through the house. Doors to
other rooms should not be on the same wall as the main door, or
aligned directly in front of it. If this is the case, keep the doors closed,
or hang a crystal between the facing doors.

Make sure that the door does not face directly on to any killing arrows
inside the house (see page 83). The main door should not face the door
to a toilet as this may sour the ch'i entering the home. If it does, always
keep the toilet door closed and consider placing a large mirror on the
toilet door to camouflage the room.

Your personal auspicious directions

In addition to all these considerations, everyone has a series of
directions which are more or less auspicious, depending on their year
of birth and their personal *kua* number. This is looked at in detail on
pages 103–108 and adds a further dimension to consideration of how to
deal with the direction of your front door. Everyone also has an

astrological sign and related element which may influence the colour and style they prefer for the main door of the house (see page 99).

Main Door Worksheet

....

MAIN DOOR FACES

....

SOURCES OF *SHA CH'I*

....

ACTION REQUIRED

....

SPACE IN FRONT OF HOUSE

....

ACTION REQUIRED

....

DOOR DIRECTION FAVOURS

....

ELEMENT RELATED TO DOOR DIRECTION

....

ACTION TO ENERGISE MAIN ELEMENT

....

ACTION TO ENERGISE SUPPORTIVE ELEMENT

....

ACTION TO ENERGISE OTHER ELEMENTS

....

DOOR STYLE

....

ACTION REQUIRED

....

....

....

....

....

....

CHAPTER 10

The Movement and Stimulation of Ch'i in the Home

The principles applied to the general circulation of ch'i are equally applicable once the ch'i moves into the house through the front door. The aim is for a continuous and meandering flow of ch'i without areas where it can settle and become stagnant, or places where it moves too fast to be beneficial. Think of the wind circulating as a gentle breeze through the home, curling sinuously around the furniture and from room to room.

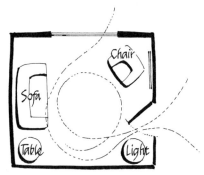

In this chapter, we will identify possible problems and mention appropriate solutions. The following chapter will give more detail on the various remedies which can be used. Remember that the solutions you consider should be appropriate for the area of the house and the area of the room in which the problem has to be resolved, and also that they must suit your own personal taste. It can never be repeated too often that balance and common sense are paramount in all your feng shui decisions.

Keep the house tidy

In a cluttered and untidy house, there is no possibility that the ch'i can have a free and even circulation. Look objectively at the furniture and possessions you keep around the home. If you are someone who only keeps the minimum of possessions, you have an easier task. If you have squirrel tendencies, it may be a good time to take a fresh look at the things you really need to hang on to. Items that you use on a regular basis or which have a strong sentimental value are obviously important to you, but hanging on to things 'in case they come in handy' usually results in a great deal of annoying clutter which very rarely comes back into use. Be ruthless and clear out unwanted junk on a regular basis. Everything you have should serve a purpose, whether it is a practical one or simply the fact that the object brings you pleasure.

If you find clearing out difficult, try undertaking the task a stage at a time. Clear one room or one cupboard, or make sure you fill one bag to be taken down to the charity shop before you give up. If you have a pile of old magazines which you dip into on a regular basis, that's fine as they are still a useful part of your life. Tidy them into a rack or container so that they are neat and easily accessible. If they are magazines you read as a teenager and are never likely to read again, don't make the mistake of thinking your own children or grandchildren are going to be interested! Throw them out.

Pay particular attention to the central section of the bagua relating to the home and to each individual room. This should be a place of calm and will be clogged by unwanted junk.

Sha ch'i

Areas where ch'i is encouraged to rush headlong through the house must be avoided. Ch'i moving too fast cannot allow its beneficial influences to settle in the room.

If there is more than one door in a line, the ch'i will move too fast. It is especially inauspicious if the front and back doors are directly opposite each other with no barrier in between. Try to keep the doors closed, and introduce screens or bead curtains or use wind chimes to moderate the flow of ch'i. You could also consider placing a small table with a vase of fresh flowers between the doors. The ch'i will then be forced to meander around the obstacle in a more leisurely way.

In each room, it is best if there are not too many doors and windows and if there is at least one solid wall, otherwise the ch'i is encouraged to rush in and out too quickly. Perhaps all the doors are not necessary, in which case they could be blocked off. Otherwise, keep them closed. Too much light from a large number of windows may also make the room too yang for its use, so think about using curtains to correct the yin/yang balance.

Look at the features of each room and make sure that they are not creating unnecessary *sha ch'i*. Are there too many sharp corners? These can cause the ch'i to change direction rapidly. Think about using wind chimes, crystals or mirrors to help deflect the ch'i into a better path. Do you have ceiling beams? These are not good feng shui as they deflect the energies into aggressive patterns and also have an oppressive effect on the people in the room. Again, use wind chimes or bamboo flutes to soften their effects.

Furniture can also create its own killing arrows. Very sharp-edged furniture should be avoided in a feng shui home. For example, dining-room and other tables are better with a softer edge, and rounded edges generally have a more auspicious effect on the energies in the room. Soften angular furniture by using trailing plants, throws, drapes or cushions. Open bookcases are a particularly strong source of killing arrows. Bookcases with doors are a better option, but if it is not possible to replace or alter furniture, as it will not be in most cases, introduce a trailing plant to hang over the front of the bookcase, or soften the effect with a small crystal or a curtain.

Si ch'i

Awkward corners, alcoves, areas blocked by furniture, narrow restrictions: all these encourage the development of pools of stagnant ch'i in the home. Look round the house and think about that gentle breeze moving through the rooms. Reposition furniture or use lights, crystals or plants to energise these areas and bring them back into the useful life of the room. The next chapter gives details of the various ways of achieving this.

Furniture positions

Especially with chairs and desks, it is best if the occupant does not sit with their back facing the door. If they do not have a view of the door, place a mirror so that they can see people entering the room.

As well as encouraging a good flow of ch'i, chairs and tables placed at an angle encourage good relationships, whereas chairs placed directly opposite each other can create a confrontational atmosphere. There is more information on furniture placement in the chapters on the individual rooms.

Stimulating ch'i

Once you have a good flow of ch'i through the house, you will want to consider areas to stimulate to improve the fortunes in your life and those of members of the family, and the chapters on separate rooms highlight this in more detail.

In each room, look at the bagua which identifies sections of the room which can be stimulated. Think about which area would be most important to energise. Is career your priority or improved relationships? Is it more important that your son has the best opportunities to continue his education or that your daughter is about to realise her ambitions in business?

Once you have made these decisions, look at the various ways in which you can encourage the ch'i in that sector to bring good fortune your way. There are a variety of symbolic objects you can use, such as wind chimes, crystals, flags, lights and plants, as you will see in the next chapter. In each case, the object or image you choose should be appropriate to the element relating to that part of the room. Always use elements which are complementary and not in opposition by relating them to the positive and negative cycles (see pages 44–5).

CHAPTER 11

Protectors and Remedies

B efore you begin to think about using objects to encourage a good flow of ch'i or to energise areas of the home, it is important to ensure that you remember the various principles established, such as the protective cycle of the elements. Using crystals, mirrors and so on thoughtfully and carefully will benefit the feng shui of your home. Using them carelessly will certainly not be helpful and could create problems which did not exist before. Move thoughtfully. You can make changes which will improve your life, but if you are already happy with the way things are going for you, be especially circumspect in your actions.

Don't go overboard with mirrors, plants and so on; always think about balance and proportion and the best position for an object in the room. Also choose items which fit with the style of your home and your own taste. There is no need to use Chinese or oriental-style objects if this is not your style.

There are a number of basic types of remedy for feng shui problems in the home. Each one has a specific function and once you have understood the principles, you can use each remedy in a variety of different circumstances.

Lights

Light is a powerful way of activating ch'i both inside and outside the home. It serves to enrich and stimulate ch'i, thus creating more positive energies. As light relates closely to fire, it is strongest in the southern part of the house or of individual rooms, but also offers good support for the qualities of earth in the south-west and north-east.

Regardless of the zone in which they occur, lights can be used to energise missing areas of the home or of a room, dispel stagnant ch'i and generate yang energies. They are ideal for lighting up the *si ch'i* which might settle in dark corners or to dissolve *sha ch'i* on sharp edges of furniture. Tall lights can also be used to regularise the shape of the home by re-energising missing corners. Light can be used anywhere where bright energy is required.

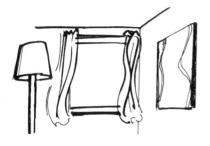

Natural light is the best source, so it is good if rooms have sufficient natural light. If not, minimise curtains and add mirrors to reflect the light. On the other hand, if there is too much light in a room, the yang can be too strong, especially in a bedroom. In that case, curtains can be used to restore the balance in favour of yin. Active rooms should be more brightly lit than those used for restful occupations. Lights should be clear and bright but never too glaring; fluorescent lighting tends to be too bright. Keep the principle of balance in mind and they can only be beneficial.

Do avoid using strong lights which are directly over people's heads, especially in areas where they sit for some time, such as at an office desk or in the living or dining room. This will have an oppressive effect. Uplighters and wall lights are an excellent way of providing ample light in a room but with a softer effect. Dimmer switches are also a good way of being able to regulate the amount of light in a room, particularly where the room has different uses. A living room, for example, may be quite lively during the day, but in the evening would benefit from a softer, more yin lighting.

Candles

Candles can also be used to provide light, but remember that it is the actual candle flame which activates the ch'i, not the candle itself, so they need to be lit and not merely included as decorative objects. Candles are a fire hazard so they should always be used with safety paramount and never left burning unattended.

Use candles in the north-east to activate the earth element, or use them in alcoves or corners (again, always safely) to energise stagnant ch'i. It is usually not a good idea to over-emphasise the fire element in the southern sectors as it can become too predominant; bear this in mind when placing candles.

Mirrors

Mirrors attract and pass on ch'i so they can be used in a number of ways.

Where a section is missing from a house or a room, they can be used to give the effect of the existence of that area, restoring the balance of the house. By deflecting *sha ch'i,* they are useful in rerouting killing arrows, while they can also enable energy to flow along a narrow or constricted passage. They can also be used to disguise areas, such as a toilet too near a main door, by making them apparently disappear. By encouraging natural light, mirrors can also help to activate and stimulate ch'i.

Another quality of mirrors is that they double the good qualities of the image they reflect, so it is important that they always reflect something pleasant. This makes them ideal for hanging in a dining room where they reflect the food on the table, and is the reason they are so often found in Chinese restaurants. It is not as good, however, if they reflect food being prepared in the kitchen. Where they reflect attractive images of nature from outside the house, this is also beneficial.

One place where they must be used with particular care is in the bedroom, as it is not good feng shui to reflect the bed itself. This will give a double image of marriage, which is not auspicious. They should also not reflect the toilet, nor should they reflect the front door as this will encourage the ch'i only just entering the house to go straight back out again.

Mirrors should be large enough to reflect a complete image, especially of a person, and ideally should allow space around them so that the image is not constrained in the mirror frame. It is not good feng shui to have them cutting off the tops of the heads of the taller members of the family. They should reflect an unbroken image, so mirror tiles or decorated mirrors are not the best feng shui, especially if they are reflecting the images of people.

Small, round convex mirrors reflect and expand ch'i energy and can be used both inside and outside the home. As they reflect an image upside-down, they can be used to remove overbearing images, such as a large neighbouring building, but should not be used where they will reflect people.

A bagua mirror, a mirror within a bagua octagon with the trigrams on the outside, should only be used outside the house. It usually shows the earlier heaven sequence which is appropriate for grave sites, so is not suitable for use inside the home. Use it only outside to deflect *sha ch'i* away from the house, but be careful where you redirect the killing arrows. Your neighbours will not thank you if you direct them at their front doors.

Crystals

Crystals are the ultimate symbol of the earth element so are most often used in the south-west, centre or north-east. They are not usually placed in the north. Clear crystals such as quartz are most commonly used, but you can also use raw minerals. Crystals encourage and disperse natural light and therefore have an uplifting effect on the ch'i energies, activating the positive and reflecting it outwards.

Hanging crystals in a window will encourage more light and energy into

the room, so they are perfect to energise dull or dark rooms, and to enliven alcoves. If they are also able to move, this is another way of stimulating energies. A faceted crystal in the window of a living room will display a yang rainbow when the light shines on to it, creating great good luck for the occupants and increasing the balance of yang, particularly suitable in a living room or playroom. As the light from the crystal redirects ch'i, they can also be used to soften *sha ch'i* on sharp corners of rooms or around sharp-edged furniture.

A solid crystal ball can be used in an appropriate position to activate specific energies. In the south-west corner or in a living room, it can be used to enhance relationships, in the north-east to stimulate the educational advancement of members of the family, or in the east to encourage successful career prospects.

Wind chimes

Wind chimes vibrate the air to stimulate and cleanse the ch'i. They can reduce negative energy and resolve conflict. To be effective, they must be placed where they will move and therefore ring to give a resonating sound which you find pleasant. Never buy a set of wind chimes unless you have heard the sound they make. Use metal chimes in metal or water areas: north, north-west and west. Use wooden chimes in wood areas: south-east and east. Use ceramic chimes in earth areas: north-east and north-west. The chimes should be hollow in order to channel the ch'i upwards, and the best chimes have six, seven, eight or nine rods.

Place wind chimes in the path of fast-moving ch'i to slow it down as they will moderate the ch'i flow, or hang them at the point where ch'i changes direction in order to smooth its path. Hanging them from a protruding beam will be beneficial in directing the energies correctly.

Chimes can be used to stimulate the luck in particular areas, such as in the west to stimulate the luck of the children of the house or in the south-west to encourage good relationships.

Moving objects

Mobiles, windmills, silk banners or flags can all be used to stimulate ch'i and encourage it to circulate, and are therefore appropriate for dealing with stagnant corners. Clocks also introduce movement into the room, which can be beneficial. They can also be placed in areas of the house which you would like to stimulate. For example, a mobile in the north-eastern corner of a child's bedroom will activate and encourage the energies relating to knowledge and education.

Plants

Plants are living objects which nourish and radiate ch'i and bring auspicious energy. They symbolise life and growth to create a fresh atmosphere. Make sure that they are always kept healthy and adequately watered. If they are flowering plants, consider their colours in relation to the elements you want to stimulate.

They can be used to stimulate ch'i which is at risk of stagnating in corners and to enliven unused spaces. Plants are ideal for softening

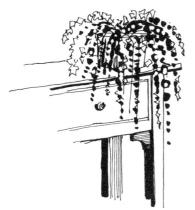

acute angles and dissolving the effect of killing arrows, especially if they are used to drape over the edges of bookcases or sharp-cornered office furniture. Sharp-leafed plants are more yang and make ch'i move more quickly. Round-leafed plants have more yin qualities. Linked with the wood element, they can be very effective in the southern parts of rooms to invigorate the fire element.

As plants are wood elements, avoid placing them in the south-west, centre and north-east, which are earth sectors. The living room and dining room are the best place for plants, and they should only be used sparingly in kitchens and bedrooms.

Cacti and spiky plants are not good if placed too near people and should certainly be avoided in the south-west, as this is the relationships zone. However, some sources say that they can be placed on window sills to deter burglars.

Artificial flowers are less effective, but can still stimulate ch'i if they are kept clean and tidy. Remember to dust them regularly. Dried arrangements are not as beneficial. If they are used, they are better kept out of reach and ideally should be seasonal in character.

Water

Water features can be used both inside and outside the home in the form of fountains, ponds, aquaria or indoor water features. They are most effective in the north, a water area, or in the east or south-east, wood areas.

Water symbolises money, and if the water feature is an aquarium containing goldfish, this is particularly good luck. Keep an odd number of fish, and make sure that one of them is black to absorb any negative energies. Place the aquarium in the south-east to activate your financial good fortune, but make sure that it is always clean and that the water is constantly moving. A stagnant aquarium will have the opposite effect.

In the north of the living room, you could keep a single bowl of water, perhaps with an image of a turtle, to strengthen the smooth nature of your journey through life.

Paintings of free-flowing, clear water can also be used to stimulate appropriate areas of the house, and can be placed on the left-hand side of the main door to stimulate good luck.

Electrical objects

In the modern world, electrical equipment such as televisions, computers, stereos and so on also serve to stimulate ch'i. They can be placed in specific sites in a room to activate the ch'i energies associated with that area. A television in the eastern section of the living room will stimulate the good health of the family and encourage a positive outlook on life.

Sound

Background noises can be either annoying or relaxing depending on the character of the noise and the atmosphere of the room. Sound adds life and yang to a room, so leaving a radio playing can restore the balance to a living room which is too strongly yin, while it would be unwelcome in a quiet reading room or peaceful bedroom. Match the level of sound to the use of the room and the needs of the occupants. Common sense is your guide here.

Heavy objects

Large and heavy objects can add stability if this is required in a particular area. Outside the house, large stones or sculptures can be used to create balance in an area, add yang and stabilise an otherwise unsettling environment. Be careful that the objects are not so large or badly placed so that they block the free passage of ch'i. Iron objects can be used to stabilise ch'i, but have a strong influence so should be used with care.

Screens, doors and curtains

Where there is too much *sha ch'i*, screens can be used to divert the ch'i flow and restore a more favourable balance. They are useful if you have a line of doors through which ch'i rushes too quickly, or to restore a regular shape to a room.

Where *sha ch'i* is created by an open bookcase, a screen or door over the bookcase will prevent the adverse *sha ch'i* from affecting the occupants of the room.

Curtains can also be used to soften *sha ch'i* by eliminating harsh corners, and their soft, yin qualities can help to restore a relaxing balance in a room which is too strongly yang. By blocking out light, they also increase the yin, which can be used to good effect. Net curtains block out inauspicious views from the windows, while still allowing light into the room.

Symbols

You can use symbolic objects to energise areas of a room, particularly in the living room. Choose an appropriate symbol for the purpose you have in mind: a red rose, for example, to energise your romance corner. If you are using symbolic objects, however, always choose items which are meaningful to you. Do not try to incorporate oriental symbols if they do not fit with your decor or with your own feelings. Sometimes, however, something from another culture strikes a chord with your own experience, so some Chinese symbols may be appropriate.

When you are using objects or images, place them in the area of the room or house which you want to stimulate. For example, place a picture of a beautiful landscape in the northern corner of a room to encourage a smooth career path, or a vase of flowers in the south-west to foster good marital relationships.

Some symbols also have an elemental association and therefore are best placed in specific areas of the house. Bamboo, for example, is a wood symbol and therefore is best used where the qualities of wood need to be supported or stimulated. In other cases, try to use an object which is made of an appropriate substance in the right areas of the house. For example, a metal turtle will be supportive in the northern sector of a room. Personal elemental associations based on your year of birth (see page 99) may also influence your choices.

You can also relate the symbols to the appropriate numbers relevant to their positions: one metal turtle in the north; two red mandarin ducks in the south-west; three fish in the east (see page 114).

The following is a list of symbols you might use and their traditional meanings.

bamboo	longevity
bat	luck and happiness
bear	strength and courage
bells	to break up negative ch'i

blossom trees	longevity
broom	to sweep away trouble
butterflies	love and joy
cannon	to combat *sheng ch'i*, a very powerful symbol to be used with care
chimera	to guard against evil
chrysanthemum	good luck
coins	prosperity
conch shell	prosperity and good luck in travel
crane	longevity and fidelity
deer	longevity and wealth
dog	protection and prosperity
dove	long life
dragon	the ultimate symbol of good luck and creativity
dragonfly	delicacy
ducks, pair of mandarin	happiness in love
eagle	farsightedness
elephant	wisdom, strength and protection
fan	protection
fish	to ward off evil
flowers	to stimulate good fortune and wealth
fountain	wealth and prosperity
fruits	to stimulate good fortune
goldfish	success and abundance
goose	trust and faithfulness in marriage
horse	speed and perseverance
ideal landscapes	to stimulate good fortune
jars	placed near the entrance to encourage ch'i to settle and accumulate
knot	a continuous knot brings never-ending good fortune
leopard	bravery
lotus	good luck grown outside the house
love birds	romance
lychees	a sweet life
monkey	cleverness and protection from bad luck
oranges	gold
orchid	good luck
peaches	long life
peacock	beauty
peony	good luck
phoenix	prosperity
pine	longevity

plum blossom	good luck
pomegranates	plenty of children
swallows	prosperity and success
swords, crossed	to combat *sheng ch'i*, a very powerful symbol to be used with care
tiger	courage
tortoise	longevity
umbrella or canopy	protection from thieves, especially near the door
waterfalls	to stimulate good fortune
wheel of law	protection

Bamboo flutes

Bamboo flutes are a potent Chinese symbol, bringing good luck and driving off evil. One way in which they can be used is to dissolve the *sha ch'i* created by beams in the ceiling. Hang a pair of bamboo flutes on overhead beams at a thirty-degree angle to represent the shape of the top of the bagua, with the mouthpieces pointing downwards. Using a red ribbon will bring additional good luck.

Pictures

Pictures are very potent symbols. They should always be chosen because they are pleasing – common sense will tell you that – but they can be placed in more or less auspicious positions according to feng shui principles.

The images actually displayed may relate to the elements or to things which are particularly symbolic. For example, the ideal place for a picture of a pair of mandarin ducks is in the south-west relationships sector. If you have a picture there of a solitary person walking along a beach, perhaps you might be better to find an alternative position for that image.

Colour

The use of colour has already been discussed in detail in chapter 6 in relation to the elements. It can be used to stimulate, support or negate elemental effects.

In addition to this, colours have different associations in the East than in the West. In the East, red is an auspicious colour which brings happiness, especially with the new year, while white is associated with mourning. Yellow indicates longevity, blue reflects the sky, and green symbolises growth and freshness. Think about linking these qualities to pictures or symbols you introduce into the home.

Your personal element based on your year of birth (see page 99) will also influence your use of colour in the home.

CHAPTER 12

Personal Birth Year Sign and Elements

Having established the general principles of feng shui which relate to direction, energies and family members, there is yet another layer of complexity which can be overlaid to improve the suitability of feng shui decisions for your personal situation.

Like Western astrology, Chinese astrology allocates a sign to each individual person depending on when they were born. The Chinese astrological calendar identifies a character type according to year of birth. There are twelve animal signs relating to the years, which rotate continuously in sequence: rat, ox, tiger, rabbit, dragon, snake, horse, goat, monkey, rooster, dog, pig.

The animals are also known as the earthly branches. They are grouped around the compass points and relate to specific compass directions and therefore to particular seasons (see page 119).

In addition to this, each year is associated with one of the elements: metal, water, wood, fire, earth. These rotate in a two-year cycle.

The earthly branches also relate to two-hour time periods during the day and to months of the year. By using complex calculations based on these movements of the earthly branches in relation to other elements, feng shui experts, like Western astrologers, can extend their calculations to include the actual date and time of birth for a more accurate reading both of your astrological sign and your elemental association. This is the province of the experts.

You can find out more about the characteristics relating to different astrological signs by reading *Tung Jen's Chinese Astrology* and *Tung Jen's Chinese Love Signs*, both published by Foulsham.

The Chinese new year

The start of the Chinese astrological year falls during January or February and varies from year to year. If you were born on or after 21

February, simply refer to your actual year of birth according to the Western calendar. If you were born between 20 January and 20 February, you must check whether to use your actual year of birth or the previous year in your calculations and to do this you will need to look up the actual date of the Chinese new year. This falls on the first new moon of the year and the dates are listed below as there is no simple mathematical way of working them out.

Year	First day of the Chinese new year	Year	First day of the Chinese new year	Year	First day of the Chinese new year
1900	31 January	1936	24 January	1972	16 February
1901	19 February	1937	11 February	1973	3 February
1902	8 February	1938	31 January	1974	23 January
1903	29 January	1939	19 February	1975	11 February
1904	16 February	1940	8 February	1976	31 January
1905	4 February	1941	27 January	1977	18 February
1906	25 January	1942	15 February	1978	7 February
1907	13 February	1943	5 February	1979	28 January
1908	2 February	1944	25 January	1980	16 February
1909	22 January	1945	13 February	1981	5 February
1910	10 February	1946	2 February	1982	25 January
1911	30 January	1947	22 January	1983	13 February
1912	18 February	1948	10 February	1984	2 February
1913	6 February	1949	29 January	1985	20 February
1914	26 January	1950	17 February	1986	9 February
1915	14 February	1951	6 February	1987	29 January
1916	3 February	1952	27 January	1988	17 February
1917	23 January	1953	14 February	1989	6 February
1918	11 February	1954	3 February	1990	27 January
1919	1 February	1955	24 January	1991	15 February
1920	20 February	1956	12 February	1992	4 February
1921	8 February	1957	31 January	1993	23 January
1922	28 January	1958	18 February	1994	10 February
1923	16 February	1959	8 February	1995	31 January
1924	5 February	1960	28 January	1996	19 February
1925	25 January	1961	15 February	1997	8 February
1926	13 February	1962	5 February	1998	28 January
1927	2 February	1963	25 January	1999	16 February
1928	23 January	1964	13 February	2000	5 February
1929	10 February	1965	2 February	2001	24 January
1930	30 January	1966	21 January	2002	12 February
1931	17 February	1967	9 February	2003	1 February
1932	6 February	1968	30 January	2004	22 January
1933	26 January	1969	17 February	2005	9 February
1934	14 February	1970	6 February	2006	29 January
1935	4 February	1971	27 January	2007	18 February

Calculating your Chinese astrological sign

To find out your personal Chinese astrological sign, take the last two digits of the year in which you were born. If the number is twelve or more, subtract twelve, and continue to subtract twelve until you have a number less than twelve. For example, if you were born in 1940, your subtraction would be as follows:

$$40 - 12 = 28$$
$$28 - 12 = 16$$
$$16 - 12 = 4$$

If the number is less than twelve already, then use that number. Refer the final number to the list below to discover your astrological sign.

Number	Animal	Group	Number	Animal	Group
0	rat	group 1	6	horse	group 3
1	ox	group 2	7	goat	group 4
2	tiger	group 3	8	monkey	group 1
3	rabbit	group 4	9	rooster	group 2
4	dragon	group 1	10	dog	group 3
5	snake	group 2	11	pig	group 4

The animals are linked into four groups, as indicated above. Each of the three signs within each group will find that they are the most compatible in terms of personal characteristics, so the best combinations are: rat, dragon and monkey; ox, snake and rooster; tiger, horse and dog; rabbit, goat and pig.

The signs also have opposites which are unlikely to be compatible. Group one and group three oppose each other; in particular the rat opposes the horse; the monkey opposes the tiger; and the dragon opposes the dog. In the same way, groups two and four have opposite signs: the ox opposes the goat; the rooster opposes the rabbit; and the snake opposes the pig.

Work out your personal sign and those of your family and fill them in on the worksheet with the compatible and incompatible signs.

Calculating your personal element

Depending on your year of birth, your personality will be affected by a particular element which will influence your environmental relationship with the elements.

To discover your personal element, take the last digit of the year in which you were born. Refer this to the list below to find your personal element.

Number	Element	Number	Element
0	metal	5	wood
1	metal	6	fire
2	water	7	fire
3	water	8	earth
4	wood	9	earth

Using your personal element

The elemental balance of zones and the use of colours and symbolic objects will be influenced by your personal element. Use this to your advantage to strengthen your personal characteristics or provide support where it is required. You can even try to temper dominant personality traits – if you tend to be an argumentative fire sign, temper the fire areas of your environment.

If you were born in an earth year, you will feel most comfortable with objects made of earth: crystals, ceramics and so on. Fire will be the element to give you support, but wood things will have a negative influence. Metal will mitigate the stability of earth, useful if you feel you are too sensible and down-to-earth. You may also feel sympathies with the elemental colours: positive towards brown and yellow, orange and red; negative towards green.

People born under the water sign are likely to be sensitive and intuitive. They will feel comfortable with water symbols, but metal may add useful strength. Wood will absorb some of the water qualities if they are too dominant, but earth will have a negative effect. Positive colours are blue, black, white, gold and silver; negative ones are brown and yellow.

The positive and challenging people born in a wood year will relate well to wood or water, finding that water symbols give them more sensitivity. Those who are over-ambitious may temper their enthusiasm with fire, but should avoid metal, which could cut them down. Colours which are most complementary are green, blue and black.

Dynamic fire people are likely to react well to strong colours – reds, oranges and purples – and avoid blue and black. If their personality is very fiery, they may need the purposeful direction of wood to support them, or even soften their passion with earth symbols. Water symbols will not find much of a place in their home.

The strong-minded metal sign will gain additional support and stability from earth, or can be tempered and given more sensitivity by water symbols. Fire will weaken their strength. White, gold, silver, blue and black are positive colours; red and orange are negative.

Personal Sign and Element Worksheet

NAME

YEAR OF BIRTH

ASTROLOGICAL SIGN

GROUP

COMPATIBLE SIGNS

OPPOSITE SIGN

PERSONAL ELEMENT

NAME

YEAR OF BIRTH

ASTROLOGICAL SIGN

GROUP

COMPATIBLE SIGNS

OPPOSITE SIGN

PERSONAL ELEMENT

NAME
....

YEAR OF BIRTH
....

ASTROLOGICAL SIGN
....

GROUP
....

COMPATIBLE SIGNS
....

OPPOSITE SIGN
....

PERSONAL ELEMENT

NAME
....

YEAR OF BIRTH
....

ASTROLOGICAL SIGN
....

GROUP
....

COMPATIBLE SIGNS
....

OPPOSITE SIGN
....

PERSONAL ELEMENT

CHAPTER 13

Your Personal Kua Number

We have already seen how specific compass directions have positive or negative implications for particular members of the family. In a similar way, each person has compass directions which are auspicious or inauspicious for them personally in specific ways. You can discover these by calculating your personal *kua* number or lucky number, which is based on your year of birth. Based on your *kua* number, four of the compass directions and locations will be auspicious for you, and four will not.

Calculating your kua number

To calculate your personal lucky number, add together the last two digits of your year of birth. Remember that if your birthday falls between 20 January and 20 February, you must check whether to use the actual year or the previous one (see page 98). If the sum is ten or more, add them together again so that you have a single digit. If you are a man, subtract that number from ten to give your personal lucky number. If you are a woman, add five to the number. If this creates a two-digit number, add those digits together to give your lucky number. For example, Tom was born in September 1966 so:

6 + 6 = 12
1 + 2 = 3
10 – 3 = 7

Jane was born in May 1969, so:

6 + 9 = 15
1 + 5 = 6
6 + 5 = 11
1 + 1 = 2

Once we move into the twenty-first century, the calculation will be slightly different to maintain the cycle of numbers. Males born in 1999 will have a *kua* number of one; females will have a *kua* number of five. Men born in the year 2000 will have a *kua* number of nine and females a *kua* number of six. The calculations will then be to add together the last two digits until you have a single digit. Men should then deduct that number from nine to give their *kua* number. Women should add four to their single-digit number.

East-group and west-group people

Once you have discovered you *kua* number, you will be able to determine whether you are an east-group or a west-group person.

East-group people have a *kua* number of one, three, four or nine. Their best directions and locations are north, east, south-east and south; their worst are therefore south-west, west, north-west and north-east.

West-group people have a *kua* number of two, five, six, seven or eight. Their best directions and locations are north-east, south-west, west and north-west. Their worst directions are therefore north, east, south-east and south.

Auspicious directions

Although the same four directions are good and bad for all east-group people and all west-group people, the type and degree of good or ill fortune associated with those directions is different for the different *kua* numbers. The four auspicious directions are: *fu wei, tien yi, nien yen* and *sheng ch'i*. The four inauspicious directions are: *ho hai, wu kwei, chueh ming* and *lui sha*.

Fu wei luck will bring you reasonable good fortune and relates in particular to your personal growth and development. *Tien yi* luck is sometimes known as the 'good doctor' as it relates to your health. *Nien yen* luck specifically refers to your progress in personal relationships, both with family and friends and with romantic partners. *Sheng ch'i* luck is the most positive direction and should bring overall success and prosperity to your life.

On the negative side, *ho hai* luck is likely to find you dealing with problems and accidents in your life and suffering frustration in trying to solve them. *Wu kwei* luck, the 'five ghosts' as it translates from the Chinese, is a quarrelsome direction likely to encourage difficult and confrontational relationships. The 'six killings' or *chueh ming* luck is a general bad-luck direction, although the worst direction is *lui sha* or 'total loss'.

Use the charts to see which are your best and worst directions according to your personal *kua* number. The directions for the central *lo shu* number, five, are different for males and females.

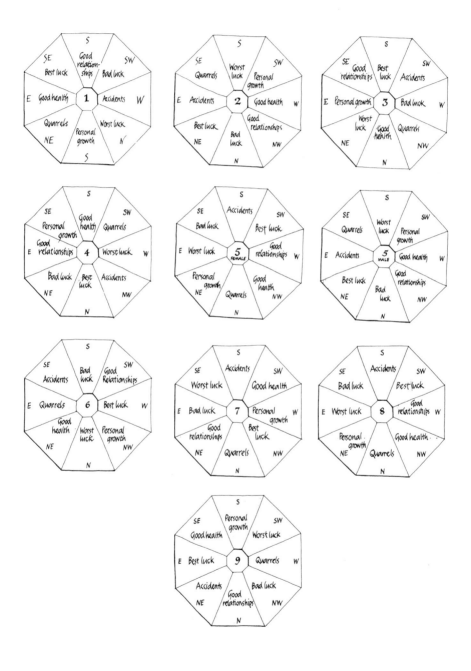

How to use your personal lucky number

Once you have established your personal lucky number, you can apply the information to your home to maximise the effects of the good luck which might come your way.

If possible, your main door should be facing one of your auspicious directions, or within the sector of one of your best directions, and you should certainly try to avoid the main door facing in your worst direction. If it does, or if it faces in one of the other three inauspicious directions, you may want to consider using another door in the house as your main door, or adding a porch or other screen to change the direction of the energies entering the house.

Arranging the main rooms in the house, such as the living room and bedroom, so that they are within the best sectors of the house will give you the best chances of good luck. Less important rooms, such as the toilet, can be placed in the worst sectors.

Use your lucky sectors of rooms and avoid the unlucky ones, placing your favourite chair, for example, in the *sheng ch'i* sector of the living room. If you have a desk, position it to face an auspicious direction, and sleep with your head pointing to a good direction. For example, for success at work, choose to face your best direction when sitting at your desk. If you are looking to improve your personal relationships, sleep with your head pointing to your good relationships direction. If you are suffering from health problems, sleep and eat facing your good health direction. Students will benefit from working facing their personal growth direction. Major activities are best undertaken in one of your best directions rather than one of those which might be inauspicious.

Compromising with partners

Clearly, if both partners have the same number, you will be totally compatible in terms of your auspicious directions. If you are both from the same group, at least your four auspicious directions coincide and it will make it easier to plan your home in order to maximise the feng shui benefits. You will only have to compromise on which of the directions combines the most auspicious directions for you both. If you are from different groups, your task will be more difficult and you will have to consider very carefully which sectors to energise for each partner. You may find that a particular house suits one partner better than the other. Obviously you will try to avoid the directions which are worst for both of you, but if a particular direction is second best for you both, it may be a better choice than a direction which is good for one but not the other.

You can copy the worksheets for other members of the family.

Kua Number Worksheet

....
NAME

....
YEAR OF BIRTH

....
KUA NUMBER

....
EAST OR WEST GROUP

Auspicious directions

....
FU WEI / PERSONAL GROWTH

....
TIEN YI / GOOD HEALTH

....
NIEN YEN / GOOD RELATIONSHIPS

....
SHENG CH'I / BEST LUCK

Inauspicious directions

....
HO HAI / ACCIDENTS

....
WU KWEI / QUARRELS

....
CHUEH MING / BAD LUCK

....
LUI SHA / WORST LUCK

....

NAME

....

YEAR OF BIRTH

....

KUA NUMBER

....

EAST OR WEST GROUP

Auspicious directions

....

FU WEI / PERSONAL GROWTH

....

TIEN YI / GOOD HEALTH

....

NIEN YEN / GOOD RELATIONSHIPS

....

SHENG CH'I / BEST LUCK

Inauspicious directions

....

HO HAI / ACCIDENTS

....

WU KWEI / QUARRELS

....

CHUEH MING / BAD LUCK

....

LUI SHA / WORST LUCK

CHAPTER 14

Life Aspirations

N ow that we have looked at the more personal elements relating to feng shui, it is appropriate to link together all the elements so far and consider your personal life aspirations and how you hope to achieve them.

Think about the eight aspects of ch'i energy discussed on pages 64–66 which represent different aspects of your life and are directed from the compass points.

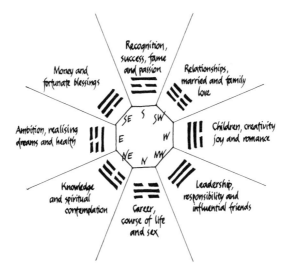

Which of these demand the most attention in your life? Number them in order of importance to you at the present time, then start with the most important aspect you have selected. You can then choose a suitable way of activating the sectors relating to that particular life aspiration. There are many ways you can do this using symbols, mirrors, lights and so on (see pages 86–96). You can also relate them to your personal *kua* number and choose to energise the most auspicious directions for you (see page 105).

Responsibility

Are qualities of leadership and the guidance of helpful friends useful and important to you at this stage in your life? Do you have a degree of responsibility and stability at work and in the family? Activate the north-western sectors or your best luck direction.

Career

The water aspect of your life relates to your own feeling of how your ship is sailing on the river of life. Are you having a choppy or a smooth passage, or are you in the doldrums? Your personal growth or best luck directions may be the best stimulus for you. Or look at the northern sectors of your home and of your living room and take action to ensure that they are in good order.

Knowledge

Are you seeking to improve your knowledge either through education or by searching for an understanding of your spiritual self? This relates to the north-east of your home and your main rooms. Also consider stimulating your personal growth direction.

Ambition

Are you pushing forward to realise your dreams? Or do they seem to be blocked at every turn? Have you recently started out in business or a new job? Stimulate eastern zones or your personal growth or best luck directions.

Money

What kind of fortunate blessings has the wind blown your way from a financial point of view? Are difficult finances the bane of your life? The south-east or your best luck directions are the areas to consider.

Recognition

Does your life lack the fire of passion and recognition for the work you put into your achievements? Is your social life in need of stimulation? Take action in the south of your home or living room or in your best luck direction.

Relationships

Are you receptive to good relationships with your partner and with others? Is this an area of your life which needs support and help? Look to the south-west areas of the home and to your good relationships direction. Make sure your bed is aligned to one of your auspicious directions and is positioned in the south-west sector of the bedroom. Symbols, such as a red rose or a pair of mandarin ducks, are especially appropriate.

Another ancient Chinese ritual designed to stimulate the chances of finding a new partner is to place a vase of fresh flowers in an auspicious part of your house and change the water daily, keeping the flowers fresh and blooming. Take the last two digits of your year of birth (referring to the Chinese years on page 98 if necessary) and keep deducting four until you have a number between nought and three. If you have a nought, place the vase in the west of your house or living room. If you are left with a one, place the vase in the south. Position it in the east if you are left with two. Place it in the north if you are left with three.

Children

Is the happiness of your children your main consideration? Are you a person who has been able to tap into the lake of creativity in your work? Perhaps you should think about energising the western sectors or your personal growth or best luck directions. Look at your relationships directions as well, as these will obviously have an effect on this area of your life.

Life Aspirations Worksheet

NAME

KUA NUMBER

RESPONSIBILITY

ACTIVATE THE NORTH-WEST OR BEST LUCK

CAREER

ACTIVATE THE NORTH, PERSONAL GROWTH OR BEST LUCK

KNOWLEDGE

ACTIVATE THE NORTH-EAST OR PERSONAL GROWTH

AMBITION

ACTIVATE THE EAST, PERSONAL GROWTH OR BEST LUCK

MONEY

ACTIVATE THE SOUTH-EAST OR BEST LUCK

RECOGNITION

ACTIVATE THE SOUTH OR BEST LUCK

RELATIONSHIPS

ACTIVATE THE SOUTH-WEST OR GOOD RELATIONSHIPS

CHILDREN

ACTIVATE THE WEST, PERSONAL GROWTH OR BEST LUCK

NAME

KUA NUMBER

RESPONSIBILITY

ACTIVATE THE NORTH-WEST OR BEST LUCK

CAREER

ACTIVATE THE NORTH, PERSONAL GROWTH OR BEST LUCK

KNOWLEDGE

ACTIVATE THE NORTH-EAST OR PERSONAL GROWTH

AMBITION

ACTIVATE THE EAST, PERSONAL GROWTH OR BEST LUCK

MONEY

ACTIVATE THE SOUTH-EAST OR BEST LUCK

RECOGNITION

ACTIVATE THE SOUTH OR BEST LUCK

RELATIONSHIPS

ACTIVATE THE SOUTH-WEST OR GOOD RELATIONSHIPS

CHILDREN

ACTIVATE THE WEST, PERSONAL GROWTH OR BEST LUCK

CHAPTER 15

The Lo Shu Square

In the introduction, we introduced the concept of the magic square which Fu Hsi recognised in the pattern on the turtle shell. Around the central number five, each of the rows of numbers add up to fifteen in any direction. This is the basic *lo shu* square.

We have seen that the numbers relate to the compass directions and therefore to other aspects of feng shui. In the same way as the magic square is divided into nine sections, so the bagua divides the house or each room within it into nine sections, relating to the eight compass directions and the centre, placing south at the top.

This creates a link between the numbers and the compass directions, trigrams and related elements. It also gives the numerical energy of the different sectors of the bagua. For example, the numerical energy of the north is one; of the south is nine, and so on. In the same way, the number one relates to 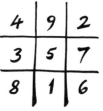 water; numbers two, eight and five to earth; numbers three and four to wood; numbers six and seven to metal and number nine to fire. If you are working to activate energies, therefore, the numbers can be significant in how you choose to achieve that.

Joining the numbers with a line in sequence creates a symbol which is used in the Jewish religion as the sign of Saturn.

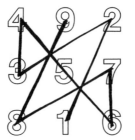

Changing cycles

In the archetypal *lo shu*, the numbers are always in the same positions around the central, 'reigning' number five and the numbers add up to fifteen in any direction. However, as the years progress, the numbers move around the square following the number sequence, so number one moves to the position of number two, number two moves to the position of number three, and so on. This is the number sequence which creates the Saturn symbol (above) and is known as the theory of the 'flying stars'.

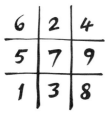

A complete cycle of the Chinese calendar lasts 180 years, but this is subdivided into periods of sixty years, which relate to the twelve astrological animals and the five elements. This interaction of heavenly and earthly symbols reflects the interdependence of heavenly and earthly forces. These sixty-year periods are again divided into three twenty-year periods and the arrangement of numbers on the *lo shu* square is different for each twenty-year period, with a different reigning number. The numbers are no longer in a 'magic' sequence. The current time period runs from 1984 to 2003 and the arrangement of numbers is based around the reigning number seven.

For houses built within this time period, the most auspicious directions are north-east, south-east and north-west. South and east are unlucky.

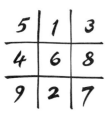

The previous time period ran from 1964 to 1983 and was ruled by the standard *lo shu* around the reigning number five. The most auspicious directions were north, north-west and north-east.

The next cycle runs from 2004 to 2023 and the *lo shu* revolves around the reigning number six. The most auspicious directions will be south and west.

The time dimension

You can also relate the numbers in the *lo shu* square to your *kua* number to determine how your fortunes will fare in a particular year. Each of the nine numbers takes its turn in the reigning position in the *lo shu* square.

Calculate the number of the current year, using the relevant gender calculation. For example, 1999 has a number of one at the centre of the grid on the male calculation. A man born in 1955 with a *kua* number of

9	5	7
8	**1**	3
4	6	2

1	6	8
9	**2**	4
5	7	3

2	7	9
1	**3**	5
6	8	4

3	8	1
2	**4**	6
7	9	5

4	9	2
3	**5**	7
8	1	6

5	1	3
4	**6**	8
9	2	7

6	2	4
5	**7**	9
1	3	8

7	3	5
6	**8**	1
2	4	9

8	4	6
7	**9**	2
3	5	1

eight, will therefore find that his personal *kua* number is in the eastern sector in 1999 and therefore it is likely to be a good year for his advancement in business and the realisation of his ambitions. A woman born in 1955 will have a *kua* number of six, while 1999 has a *kua* number of five by the female calculation. In the *lo shu* square with five in the centre, the number six appears in the north-west sector. This should be a good year for her relationships with influential people in her life.

CHAPTER 16

The Feng Shui Ruler

Like the golden section devised by the Ancient Greeks to ensure perfect proportion, the feng shui ruler shows how perfect balance and proportion can be achieved in the measurements of any objects from doors and windows to pictures and note paper. It also involves a dimension of good and bad luck.

As with the auspicious directions, each cycle of measurement, which covers 43 cm (17 in), is divided into four good and four bad sections. Use the measurements to tap into good fortune wherever possible.

For the most auspicious feng shui, look to fill your house with objects with the luckiest dimensions.

Chai

The first segment, *chai*, runs from 0 to 5.4 cm (0–2⅛ in) and is an auspicious measurement. It can be subdivided into quarters, the first bringing financial good fortune, the second indicating crystals or jewels, the third six types of good luck and the fourth abundance.

Pi

The second segment, *pi*, is inauspicious and generally relates to ill-health. It measures from 5.4 to 10.8 cm (2⅛–4¼ in). The quarters of *pi* can bring a loss of money, legal problems, general bad luck or the ill-health of a partner.

Li

Li runs from 10.8 to16.2 cm (4¼–6⅜ in) and is the second bad luck measurement relating to separation.

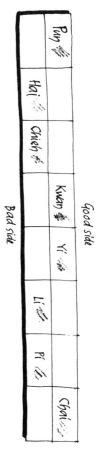

The first quarter indicates that you will be separated from good luck, the second that you will be parted from your money, the third that good friends will desert you and you may be surrounded by unscrupulous people, the fourth that you will be separated from your possessions through theft.

Yi

Yi is the second auspicious section and measures 16.2–21.5 cm (6⅜–8½ in). *Yi* attracts helpful people into your life. Good luck for your children is associated with the first quarter, unexpected income with the second, success for your son with the third quarter and general good fortune with the last quarter.

Kwan

The measurements 21.5–27 cm (8½–10⅝ in), *kwan*, offer good luck related to power. Success in exams, particular good fortune, improved income and recognition for the family are the particular aspects of the four quarters.

Chieh

Chieh does not bring good luck: 27–32.4 cm (10⅝–12¾ in) is an inauspicious measurement denoting loss. An unhappy departure is indicated by the first quarter, the loss of things you need by the second, a loss of respect by the third, and a loss of money by the fourth.

Hai

The measurements 32.4–37.5 cm (12¾–14¾ in) denote severe bad luck arriving in the form of major problems in the first quarter, ill-health in the second and third, and arguments in the fourth.

Pun

The final section, *pun*, brings good luck: 37.5–43.2 cm (14¾–17 in). It should bring money in the first quarter, good examination results in the second, jewellery or general earth luck in the third and general prosperity in the fourth.

CHAPTER 17

The Heavenly Stems and the Earthly Branches

F or the purposes of this introductory book, we have been using feng shui directions based on the eight basic compass directions. Feng shui masters, however, use a *lo pan*, or feng shui compass, which is divided into twenty-four directions. In this compass, each of the eight basic compass directions which we have been using is further subdivided into three, giving the twenty-four divisions in all. In this chapter, we will look at these divisions in outline to give you some insight into how complex the study of feng shui can become.

The divisions are made up of what are known as heavenly stems and earthly branches, with four of the eight trigrams. Each of the directions is either yin or yang, three yin directions alternating with three yang directions.

The trigrams which are used as divisions on the feng shui compass are positioned at the intercardinal points: *k'un* (south-west), *chi'en* (north-west), *ken* (north-east) and *hsun* (south-east).

The earthly branches

Around the compass, there are twelve earthly branches. Each one is associated with one of the Chinese astrogical animals.

Number	Chinese name	Animal	Direction	Season
1	*tzu*	rat	north	winter
2	*ch'ou*	ox		
3	*yin*	tiger		
4	*mao*	rabbit	east	spring
5	*chen*	dragon		
6	*ssu*	snake		
7	*wu*	horse	south	summer
8	*wei*	goat		
9	*shen*	monkey		

10	*yu*	rooster	west	autumn
11	*hsu*	dog		
12	*hai*	pig		

They are also allocated to the months of the year, days within a month and two-hour divisions of the day. They can therefore be used to give information about the right time to take specific action, depending on the compass direction in which the branches are facing at a particular time. As they are associated with the months of the year, they are also associated with the seasons.

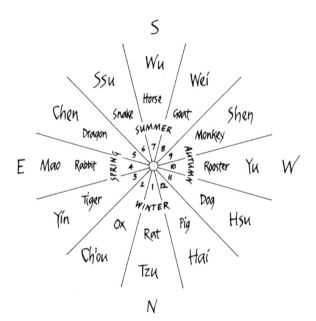

The heavenly stems

In total, there are ten numbered heavenly stems, each one relating to a particular element.

Number	Chinese name	Element	Number	Chinese name	Element
1	*chia*	wood	6	*ch'i*	earth
2	*i*	wood	7	*keng*	metal
3	*ping*	fire	8	*hsin*	metal
4	*ting*	fire	9	*jen*	water
5	*wu*	earth	10	*kuei*	water

Numbers one, two, nine and ten are associated with the *ch'ien* and *k'un* trigrams. Because these trigrams are either yin or yang rather than a balance of the two, the stems are considered unlucky. One and nine are independent and must extend their self-reliance using strong yang capabilities. Two and ten are opposite and relate to yin emptiness.

Three, four, seven and eight are associated with *ken* and *hsun*, both of which have a mixture of yin and yang and are considered lucky. Three and seven represent yang prosperity. Five and six represent the centre and are not related to a particular direction.

The twenty-four compass directions

The four trigrams, twelve earthly branches and eight heavenly stems (discounting those relating to the centre), are the twenty-four divisions of the feng shui compass, or *lo pan*.

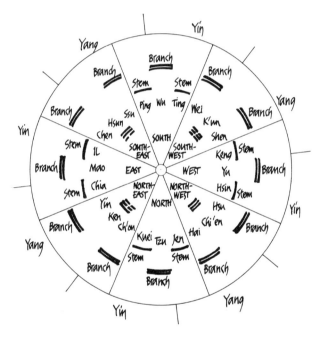

The professional lo pan

The *lo pan* used by feng shui masters may have as many as thirty-six rings set into a wooden base with a compass in the centre, although some have only seven rings. The inner ring contains the eight trigrams. The second ring contains the eight numbers of the *lo shu* square; the ninth, central number is not included. The third ring contains the twelve earthly branches. The fourth ring contains the twenty-four directions of the Chinese compass. The fifth ring contains the twenty-four divisions of the solar calendar. The sixth ring contains the sixty dragons: five of the heavenly stems with the twelve earthly branches; the sixty-year time cycles are based on this combination. The final ring contains twenty-eight constellations.

CHAPTER 18

Assessing Individual Rooms

Now you have reached the stage at which you can work through individual rooms. Because the process is the same for each one, this chapter goes through the sequence you should consider, then each of the following chapters highlights only those specific aspects you will be dealing with in that room. Jot down your thoughts on the worksheets as you are reading. Write in pencil so that you can adjust your plans as you proceed. Because these chapters are pulling together the principles you have learned, the subjects themselves will already be familiar to you.

Make a room plan

Make a plan of the room by enlarging the section of the house floor plan. Mark on the doors and windows and align the plan with the correct compass direction.

Refer to pages 49–50 for more detail.

Tidy the room

Clutter of any sort is not good feng shui as it blocks the centre of the room, which should be clear, and discourages the free flow of ch'i. Before you do anything else, tidy up the room and get rid of all unnecessary clutter and rubbish, especially in the centre.

Refer to pages 82–3 for more detail.

Deal with missing areas

If the room is an irregular shape, think about how you will compensate for the missing areas and mark these on the plan.

Refer to pages 69–72 for more detail.

Position the furniture

Think about the position of the furniture and pencil it in on the plan.

Remember to consider placing special items of furniture in the most auspicious section of the room to align them with best luck directions. For example, if the father of the house has a favourite chair, this could usefully be positioned in the north-west of the room. Avoid placing furniture so that whoever sits there will have their back to the door.

Refer to page 84 for more detail.

Avoid sha ch'i and si chi

Check the flow of ch'i through the room and make sure that it is able to move gently and freely. If there are any killing arrows, take steps to eliminate them or mitigate their effects. If there are areas of *sha ch'i*, reposition furniture or energise in other ways.

Refer to pages 83–4 for more detail.

Think about yin and yang

Balance yin and yang in an appropriate way to suit the room's use.

Refer to pages 40–2 for more detail.

Consider the qualities of energy

Think about the qualities of the energy in each section of the room and how this affects the activities within it. If relevant, relate the sectors to the members of the family. You may want to stimulate particular areas in order to help bring about changes in your life.

Refer to pages 63–6 for more detail.

Make sure the elements are in harmony

Check that the objects, symbols and colours in each sector are appropriate to the dominant element. If necessary, stimulate or soften the effects of elements within the room.

Refer to pages 44–7 for more detail.

Personalise the room

Make sure the room is appropriate for the member of the family who will most use it. For example, check the alignment of beds or desks and the use of colour. Refer to your personal *kua* number and element.

Refer to chapters 12 and 13 for more detail.

CHAPTER 19

Hallways

C h'i enters primarily through the main door of the house into the entrance hall, so it is an important room in feng shui. It then moves through the home along the passageways, so it is essential that the ch'i finds a free-flowing route so that it can move smoothly and effectively between the rooms in your home.

The entrance hall

The best entrance halls are wide enough to allow the ch'i to settle and accumulate before moving off into the house. This does not mean the area must be huge in order to ensure good feng shui, but if it is a very small area it is particularly important to keep it uncluttered and to light it well. All halls should be kept clear and tidy otherwise they will encourage stagnant ch'i and encourage feelings of apathy and tiredness.

Because the entrance hall is not a focus for family activity, it requires an even balance of yin and yang, both in the decor and in the lighting. If the hall is very light and angular, soften the effect with subtle colours and curtains or lower the level of light. If the hall is rather dark, choose slightly stronger colours, light it effectively but not harshly and hang some rectangular pictures on the walls.

Door mats can be used to welcome the ch'i into the house. Choose a colour which suits the direction in which the door faces: red for south-facing, brown for south-west-facing and so on. You could also choose the supportive element colour and use green in the south or red in the south-west and so on. Some feng shui practitioners advise that placing three golden coins under the mat will bring good fortune. Choose the Chinese coins which have a hole in the centre and tie them together with lucky red ribbon.

Another feng shui tip which can encourage good luck to come into the house is to have a bright light just inside and outside the main door.

Hallways and corridors

From the entrance hall, the ch'i flows through the house along the halls and corridors in much the same way that it flows through the energy meridians of the body. As with all ch'i flow, it is therefore especially important to ensure that it is able to move in a free-flowing but not frantic way. Ch'i rushing down long, uninterrupted corridors can lead to feelings that you do not have enough time to do anything and can therefore create tension. On the other hand, if ch'i is allowed to stagnate in corners of hallways, it can have the effect of making the occupants feel tired and apathetic. Always look out for killing arrows created by angular furniture.

As with the entrance hall, make sure hallways are clear and maintain an even yin/yang balance, using fairly neutral colours for the decor.

Correcting the movement of ch'i

In long, narrow halls down which ch'i is moving too fast, place mirrors alternately along the walls so that the ch'i is reflected from side to side and moves in a zig-zag route along the hall rather than rushing straight down the centre.

If there is a window along the side of the hall, it can be left open to encourage the ch'i to move towards it rather than rush past. Plants placed carefully along the sides of the hall will also nourish the ch'i and 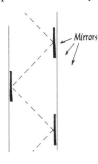 encourage a slower movement, although you should not use too many plants otherwise this can upset the even yin/yang balance you are aiming for.

If the hallway is particularly wide, doors or windows along each side should be kept closed, otherwise this will slow down the ch'i even further. Crystals hanging along the centre of the hallway will focus and speed up the ch'i flow.

Stairs

Spiral staircases are not particularly good feng shui, especially in the centre of a room, as they encourage the ch'i to follow the same path and corkscrew from one level to another. Hang a wind chime at the top and bottom of the stairs to moderate the flow.

If the stairs run directly up from the main front door, try to adjust the bottom step so that they are not immediately facing one another. If this is not possible, again hang a wind chime to moderate the flow of ch'i so that it does not by-pass the hall and rush straight up the stairs. Sometimes a screen can be erected between the stairs and the main door. If there are no other options, ensure that both the top and bottom of the stairs are very well lit to lift the energy and transform it into healthy energy.

Stairs should ideally have solid steps otherwise the ch'i will seep through the staircase and deprive the upper storey of potentially auspicious energies.

Toilets

If there is a toilet door near the main door, this can have the effect of souring the ch'i entering the house and creating a stale atmosphere. Make sure the toilet door is always kept shut, and disguise the room by placing a mirror on the outside of the door.

Hallways Worksheet

Remember the feng-shui principles repeated on pages 122–3 while you complete the worksheet on the hallways.

Room plan

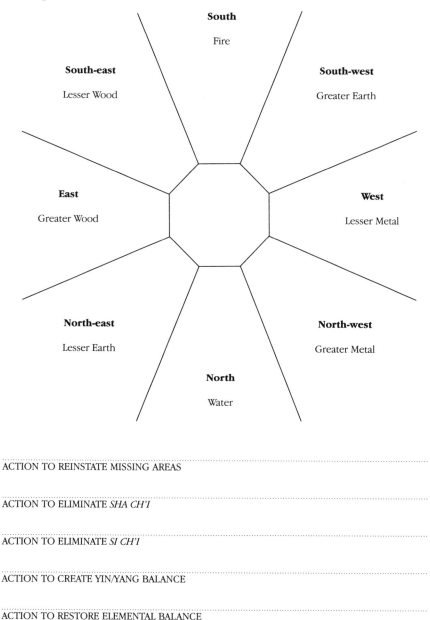

....
ACTION TO REINSTATE MISSING AREAS

....
ACTION TO ELIMINATE *SHA CH'I*

....
ACTION TO ELIMINATE *SI CH'I*

....
ACTION TO CREATE YIN/YANG BALANCE

....
ACTION TO RESTORE ELEMENTAL BALANCE

....
AREAS TO ENERGISE

CHAPTER 20

The Living Room

The living room is the heart of most homes so getting the right feng shui atmosphere here is vital. It is a place for family activity and interaction, but also a room where the strains of everyday life can be forgotten and the family can relax and enjoy each other's company in a pleasant atmosphere.

Completeness of energy qualities

It is important that the shape of the living room is regular and allows for each of the main sectors of the room to be in balance. If the room has an irregular shape, deal with this first so that you achieve a basic harmony between the major life areas. Refer back to pages 67–72.

Flow of ch'i

Look at how the ch'i can flow round the room. Are there alcoves which might encourage *si ch'i* to stagnate? Enliven them with crystals and use a mirror on protruding walls to give them a feeling of depth. Nourish stagnant ch'i in corners by placing a plant in the wasted space.

If the ceiling is uneven or has beams across it, the beams may disrupt the ch'i flow and prevent those in the room from feeling comfortable and relaxed. Position bamboo flutes tied with red ribbon on the beams, or dissipate negative ch'i with wind chimes or mobiles. Make sure they are made of the right element to harmonise with the area of the room in which they are placed.

The main door

The sector in which the door is positioned will lose some of its natural ch'i as this will move out of the door. For example, if the door is in the north-western sector, family relationships may be affected adversely. To redress this imbalance, hang a wind chime or mobile near the doorway.

Furniture placement

Is the furniture placed in such a way as to encourage a free flow of ch'i? It is best if sofas or chairs do not have their backs to the door, otherwise the occupants cannot see people entering the room. Rearrange the furniture or use mirrors to give a view of the door. Place special items of furniture, such as your favourite chair, in the sector of the room most relevant to you. Select a furniture arrangement which is harmonious rather than confrontational; imitating the shape of the bagua is a good option from a feng shui point of view as it encourages good social interaction.

Remember that the central area of the room is best kept clear of furniture and clutter. If you have a central low table in the room, place a vase of fresh flowers on it, preferably yellow in colour, to nourish the ch'i and encourage the well-being of the whole family. A plant on the window sill will also draw ch'i into the room.

Beware of killing arrows created by open bookcases or other angular furniture. Soften the effects by using bookcases with doors, or deflect the arrows with trailing plants or curtains.

Yin and yang

The balance of yin and yang is usually slightly in favour of yang in a living room as it is a place of life and activity, but make sure that if you use the room for relaxation, the yang influence is not too strong. A blend of strong shapes and softer curtains, and more neutral as well as stronger colours will help to achieve a comfortable balance. If the furniture is too angular, encouraging an excess of yang, soften the effect with throws or cushions. Encourage as much natural light as possible and make sure the overall lighting is ample but not harsh. Using dimmer switches and table lamps so that the level of light is adjustable will enable you to correct the balance depending on whether you are engaged in family activities or relaxing. Avoid having lights directly over chairs as this will be oppressive. Use soft-leafed rather than spiky plants to nourish ch'i.

Electrical equipment

The television and stereo will strongly stimulate the yang elements in the area in which they are placed. Position them carefully to benefit from the stimulation of energies. If they are in the south-east, for example, they should encourage wealth and prosperity; in the south-west they will help with good personal relationships and practicality; in the south, they will be good for your social life and recognition outside the family. If there are no particular aspects you wish to emphasise, the north or north-west of the room are sound places to position them. Remember, however, that too much stimulation will be unsettling and prevent good communication. Switch off the television when it is not being watched and learn to value silence as well as peaceful or vibrant music when the occasion demands.

The elements

Have you considered the elements in relation to the colour and objects you have placed around the room? Make sure that you enhance the qualities of individual areas: wooden objects will enhance growth potential in the south-east, for example, while water symbols will add support to the element. On the other hand, too much red in the west or north-west is negative and will create feelings of tension and undermine the strength of the males in the household. You also need to avoid too heavy an emphasis on one element. If your northern sector is all blue and black with a large aquarium, you may feel that you are drowning rather than following a buoyant path through life. Remember that balance is all-important. Instead, place your aquarium in the south-east, where the water will stimulate your wealth luck. The eastern sector is a good area for your plants. Think about the colours chosen for the decor and make sure they are in harmony with the elemental associations in the room.

Stimulating specific areas

The living room is a good location to choose if you want to stimulate particular areas of your life. Perhaps you are looking to improve your social life, in which case you could energise the southern sector with a crystal, lights or a symbolic object. Using candles – not just for decoration – is a good way to energise a room. If you have plans which you are hoping to bring to fruition, stimulate the eastern section of the room. When you are hanging pictures or placing ornaments, think about the images they represent and which areas of your life they would most enhance. Avoid images which evoke feelings of loneliness or separation, for example, in the north-western sector; instead choose pairs of objects or happy scenes. Ideal landscapes or water pictures are well positioned in the northern sector, encouraging a smooth journey through life.

A vase of flowers can stimulate the ch'i in the living room quite markedly, but they must always be kept fresh and the water must be changed regularly. Increase your social standing by placing the flowers in the south, using predominantly red and orange shades; or encourage your creativity and support the children in the family by placing white flowers in the west.

Movement can also be used to stimulate areas, and clocks provide twenty-four-hour energy.

If the room has a fireplace, it is best if it is not in the north-western or western part of the room as this will undermine the strength of the family. If your fireplace is here, balance the effect with additional water symbols in the north. Make sure that when the fire is not in use, it is kept clean and swept. Place a plant in the grate when the fire is not in use to nourish the ch'i and make sure that it is not led out of the room up the chimney.

Open-plan rooms

If you have an open-plan room which combines a living and dining area, try to take steps to make a separation between the two uses, otherwise there is a danger that neither room will be complete and you will lose certain areas of ch'i energy. Use screens, or position furniture in such a way as to create a division between the two areas, then deal with them separately as living room and dining room.

Since the dining table is the central pivot of the dining room, this does not make a good room divider in itself. This would upset the balance of both rooms as you would not be able to complete either one.

The Living-room Worksheet

Remember the feng shui principles repeated on pages 122–3 while you complete the worksheet on the living room.

Room plan

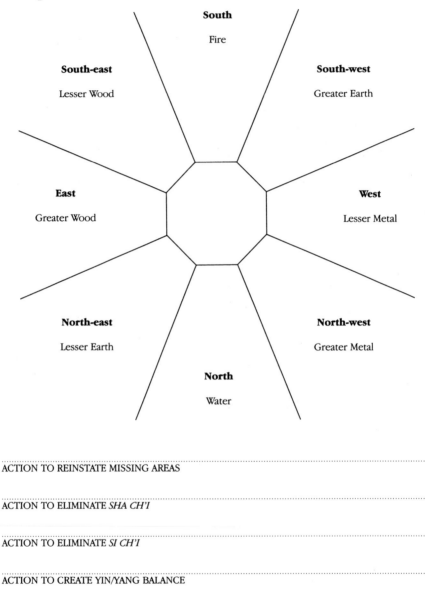

South

Fire

South-east

Lesser Wood

South-west

Greater Earth

East

Greater Wood

West

Lesser Metal

North-east

Lesser Earth

North-west

Greater Metal

North

Water

ACTION TO REINSTATE MISSING AREAS

ACTION TO ELIMINATE *SHA CH'I*

ACTION TO ELIMINATE *SI CH'I*

ACTION TO CREATE YIN/YANG BALANCE

ACTION TO RESTORE ELEMENTAL BALANCE

ACTION TO BALANCE DOOR POSITION

*Areas to energise with symbols or placement of
special furniture*

IN THE NORTH-WEST / FATHER / RESPONSIBILITY / GREATER METAL

IN THE NORTH / MIDDLE SON / CAREER / WATER

IN THE NORTH-EAST / YOUNGEST SON / KNOWLEDGE / LESSER EARTH

IN THE EAST / ELDEST SON / AMBITION / GREATER WOOD

IN THE SOUTH-EAST / ELDEST DAUGHTER / WEALTH / LESSER WOOD

IN THE SOUTH / MIDDLE DAUGHTER / RECOGNITION / FIRE

IN THE SOUTH-WEST / MOTHER / RELATIONSHIPS / GREATER EARTH

IN THE WEST / YOUNGEST DAUGHTER / CHILDREN / LESSER METAL

CHAPTER 21

The Kitchen

The kitchen is where the family's food is prepared, giving them the strength to go out and work for a higher level of prosperity. For this reason, it is said to govern the wealth of the family. Establishing a balanced and auspicious level of ch'i in the kitchen will ensure that the food prepared in that room will also be balanced and the benefits of this will be passed on to those who eat it. The best positions for the kitchen are in the east, south-east or north of the house.

The kitchen door

The door to the kitchen should open as freely as possible, as a well-proportioned entrance will ensure the optimum flow of ch'i into this important room. Try not to block the movement of the door by placing a cupboard or fridge, for example, immediately behind it.

Keeping the room tidy

A cluttered kitchen often reflects a cluttered state of finances in the family as the kitchen is rooted in the water element which symbolises wealth, so it is important to keep the kitchen clear of obstructions and to avoid having work surfaces littered with bits and pieces. If the state of your kitchen reflects the state of your finances, then can you think of a better reason to get on with that spring clean you have been promising yourself?

Remember that *sha ch'i* will be created by angular or open shelves or other sharp objects, and this must be avoided. If you do have open shelves, try to use rounded containers and avoid books having their spines directly facing the cook, as this can be detrimental to health.

The position of the oven

The position of the oven should allow a clear view of the door and the person cooking should not feel cramped. If they do, this indicates that the ch'i is not flowing smoothly. Mirrors or heat-resistant reflective metal can be used to create an effective illusion of space and therefore encourage a more relaxed atmosphere. It is best if the oven and the sink, or the oven and the fridge, are not immediately adjacent, as the elemental associations clash. Ideally, the oven should not be in the northern part of the room, as fire clashes with water, nor in the north-western sector. This is because the symbol of the north-west is heaven and positioning a fire at heaven's gate will result in poor success for the head of the family.

The water features

The north, with its associations with water, is the ideal zone for the sink, although for most people the sink position is governed by practicalities.

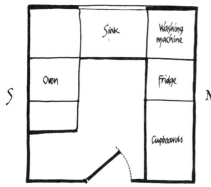

The only zone which is not really suitable is the south. If the sink cannot be in the northern sector, perhaps the washing machine or dishwasher can be placed there as another way of stimulating a good career path. Both these items should run as quietly as possible so that they do not upset the surrounding ch'i. If they are aggressively noisy, they may well have adverse effects. Positioned in the south-west, for example, they could disrupt family relationships, or in the east they could have adverse effects on the health of the family.

Electrical equipment

Items of electrical equipment in the kitchen, such as the fridge and the microwave, run constantly so are the perfect way to stimulate particular areas of the room. Place the fridge in the south-eastern wealth sector to improve your financial position still further, or in the south-west to encourage good family relationships. Try to avoid placing the fridge in the south, as the fire element is incompatible with the cool temperatures. The microwave is easily portable, so you can choose which sector is most appropriate for stimulation in this way. The north-west or western zones associated with metal receive extra stimulation if the microwave is placed there. Smaller electrical items, such as kettles, blenders and so on, are even more portable and can be used in different sectors to ensure ch'i stimulation throughout the areas. If it is possible for the energy socket which feeds the appliance to be positioned facing one of your auspicious directions, that is even better.

The position of the kitchen clock can be calculated to stimulate particular zones: the tranquil north or the passionate south, for example, depending on your circumstances.

Yin and yang

Because the kitchen is a scene of activity and life, the ideal atmosphere will be predominantly yang. Wood favours yin while metal emphasises yang, so balance these opposites appropriately for your circumstances. An excess of the former could lead to a lethargic spirit in the family; an excess of the latter could make them unable to relate to each other emotionally.

Lighting and colour

Good, but not harsh, lighting is important. Natural light brings the best ch'i into the kitchen, so single-paned windows without divisions which block out natural light are best. Keep curtains well back from the windows or use blinds and keep them raised during daylight hours. Only keep a plant or a crystal on the window sill to nourish and energise the ch'i; don't clutter the area with bits and pieces. If the kitchen is small and tends to be rather dark, make sure that the walls are painted in a light colour and that the level of light is sufficient to ensure a good atmosphere.

Colours can be fairly vibrant, perhaps taking their cue from the sector element so that you can stimulate the ch'i by referring to the positive cycle of the elements.

Plants and herbs

The best plants to grow in a kitchen are fresh herbs. Not only will they energise the sector in which they are placed, or encourage solar ch'i to enter the room, they will provide a spiritual boost to those eating the food with which they are prepared.

Kitchen-dining rooms

With all rooms, it is best if they are kept as separate as possible, otherwise each room has a section missing from its ch'i energies.

If possible, construct a partition or wall to divide the two rooms and give them their own independent ch'i. If this is not possible a screen or breakfast bar between the two rooms, with two plants at the meeting point, can serve to separate the sections. Since a table is the focus of the dining room, this is not the best item to use as a dividing partition (see page 140).

The Kitchen Worksheet

Remember the feng shui principles repeated on pages 122–3 while you complete the worksheet on the kitchen.

Room plan

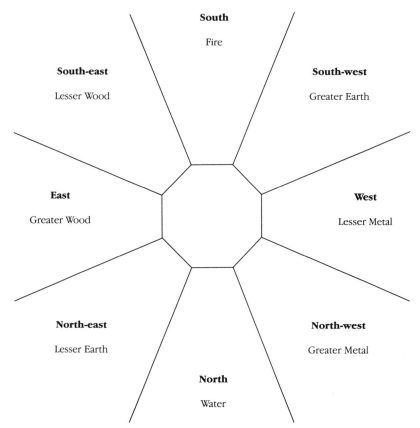

ACTION TO REINSTATE MISSING AREAS

ACTION TO ELIMINATE *SHA CH'I*

ACTION TO ELIMINATE *SI CH'I*

ACTION TO CREATE YIN/YANG BALANCE

ACTION TO RESTORE ELEMENTAL BALANCE

BEST POSITION OF OVEN

BEST POSITION OF SINK

BEST POSITION OF WASHING MACHINE

BEST POSITION OF FRIDGE

BEST POSITION OF MICROWAVE

BEST POSITION OF OTHER ELECTRICAL EQUIPMENT

BEST POSITION OF CLOCK

AREAS TO ENERGISE

CHAPTER 22

The Dining Room

Both in the East and in the West, dining is considered a social experience, and good feng shui in the dining room will help to ensure that the family enjoys sound and strong relationships, forming a firm foundation for their success in all areas of their lives. The ideal position for the dining room is therefore as near as realistically possible to the centre of the house.

The dining-room door

The door of the dining room should open on to as spacious an area as possible so that the diners feel relaxed. If the door is opposite a wall, a mirror or attractive picture will help to give an illusion of depth and have a similar effect. The position of the dining-room door often has an effect on how people feel when they enter the room. If it is in the north-west, they will feel secure; if it is in the east they will feel optimistic. Because it governs energy and passion, the southern zone is not the best position for the door, although any negative effects can be minimised by hanging a wind chime over the door.

Lighting and mirrors

A relaxed atmosphere will be encouraged by a feeling of spaciousness, so high-ceilinged rooms make good dining rooms. Encourage a feeling of height and space by using uplighters around the walls. Too bright lighting is too strongly yang and will not encourage a relaxed atmosphere, so choose dimmer switches or use smaller lights so that you can select a suitable level of lighting. Candlelit dinners are excellent, as the candles energise the ch'i around the table and the guests.

Mirrors are also excellent feng shui in the dining room as they can not only increase the levels of natural light and give an illusion of a more spacious room but they also double the abundance on the table and make any events appear twice as impressive and productive. This creates a very positive charge in the environmental and personal ch'i of those in the room.

Yin and yang

Because dining is a relaxed and social activity, the balance should be slightly in favour of yin, with softer lighting and more muted colours than in the living room. Try to avoid furniture which is too sharp-edged, as this is too strongly yang and will make guests feel overactive and unable to relax. On the other hand, overstuffed chairs or very dark, heavy curtains may make them too passive. You are aiming for a comfortably relaxed atmosphere, but still with lively conversation, so go for balance.

Colours and the elements

Colours should be more muted than strident in order to achieve the right balance. If you wish to stimulate particular areas of the room, small splashes of an appropriate colour are all that is needed. A relatively small red ornament in the south-west will add support to the earth qualities in that sector, for example, or a blue picture enhance the career prospects if placed in the north.

The table

Choose as large a table as is reasonable for the size of room and the number of people who usually use it. Having space at the table gives a feeling of abundance and maintains a good balance of bodily ch'i. Feeling cramped while eating can lead to tension and digestive disorders. As the table is the dominant piece of furniture in the room, its shape will influence the remaining furniture. If you have a round or oval table, then the rest of the furniture should be more square or rectangular. If the table is rectangular, then choose some more rounded pieces of furniture to complement it, such as a round trolley or coffee table. Wood is the best choice for a dining table as it has a strong yin quality which is conducive to good dining.

Position the table in a sector appropriate to the circumstances. If the meals are mainly enjoyed by family members, then the south-west or west are good choices as they relate to family relationships and children. For business entertaining, the north or north-west would be the better positions as they influence positive career progression and leadership qualities.

Tableware

Simply shaped crockery is the best to choose, although octagonal plates simulating the shape of the bagua are good feng shui. Metal cutlery should be well polished so that it stimulates the ch'i energies. The colour of table linen can be chosen to match the area in which you have placed the table: blue in the north, green in the east, and so on. If you always use a white cloth, think about having appropriately coloured napkins. If you have a round table, choose round tablemats, or use rectangular ones on a rectangular table. Again, select the colours to suit the sector, either complementary or supportive. Because it activates the ch'i energy, crystal glassware is an excellent choice as it provides each diner with a personal crystal to energise them throughout the meal.

Plants and ornaments

Avoid spiky plants in the dining room as these will make people feel too energetic and prevent them from relaxing. Choose specimens with gently rounded foliage, although not so soft and floppy that they encourage a feeling of lethargy. Flowers can be used to stimulate the ch'i on the table and you can make a good choice by selecting a colour to suit the element for that sector of the room.

An aquarium with small, active fish is well sited in a dining room, although it should not be in the southern, fire sector as the elements will clash. This will bring both movement and life into the room.

If you are eating with close friends or family, the conversation will be quite enough sound stimulation for the surrounding ch'i. However, if you are entertaining new acquaintances or business colleagues, a little background music can help to smooth the flow of ch'i as it will serve to relax the guests' bodily ch'i, and also to even out any lulls in the conversation. Make sure that you play something which does not challenge the tastes of those present. Quiet, instrumental music is generally therapeutic and conducive to good conversation. Clocks are better kept out of the dining room as their constant movement and reminder of the passage of time clashes with the positive symbolism of food and eating.

Seating plans

The most important guest should always be asked to sit at the head of the table, preferably facing the door, although if this is not possible a mirror should give a good view of the door. Other members of the family can best take their places in the relevant sector around the table: the father in the north-west, mother in the south-west, sons in the east, north and north-east and daughters in the south-east, south and west.

The Dining-room Worksheet

Remember the feng shui principles repeated on pages 122–3 while you complete the worksheet on the dining room.

Room plan

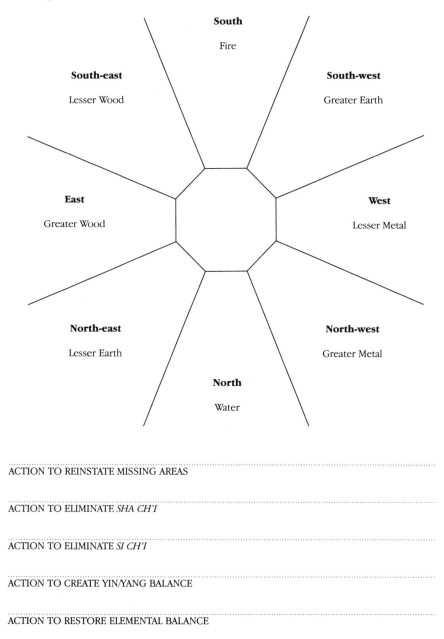

ACTION TO REINSTATE MISSING AREAS

ACTION TO ELIMINATE *SHA CH'I*

ACTION TO ELIMINATE *SI CH'I*

ACTION TO CREATE YIN/YANG BALANCE

ACTION TO RESTORE ELEMENTAL BALANCE

ACTION TO BALANCE DOOR POSITION

POSITION OF DINING TABLE

STYLE AND SHAPE OF TABLE

CROCKERY AND TABLEWARE

AREAS TO ENERGISE

CHAPTER 23

The Study or Office

Since the south-west dominates wealth, the north career progress, the north-west leadership and responsibility, and the north-east knowledge, you have plenty of choices on where in the house to site your study or home office. All these areas offer auspicious ch'i energies for your activities. Activate the appropriate elements of metal for strength, earth for knowledge or wood for ambition.

If the room is not in the ideal part of the house, think about the elemental associations of the sector in which it does fall and use the strengths of appropriate elements in the placement of the furniture and the style of the room.

Stimulation of special zones of the room can be achieved using lights or crystals, or by placing the computer or other electrical equipment in an appropriate part of the room: the north to enhance a smooth career path; the east to bring your ambitions to fruition.

Yin and yang

As this is a place of activity and stimulation, the balance should be in favour of yang. This is likely to occur naturally as office furniture tends to be more angular, there is likely to be a computer and a telephone or other electrical equipment and you will most likely choose stronger rather than pastel colours. Blinds will also increase the yang, rather than heavy curtains.

Encourage as much natural light as possible, and make sure that the room generally is well lit. This is not only practical, but activates the surrounding energies and encourages a purposeful working environment. Be careful that an overhead light is not positioned directly above the person sitting at the desk, otherwise this will create negative mental pressure.

The placement of the desk

The person sitting at the desk should have a clear view of the door and be aligned with one of the occupant's auspicious directions (see pages 103–107). You can also try to place the desk in an appropriate sector of the room to gain the most benefit from the qualities of the energy. If the room is small and the desk has to be placed with the person's back to the door, hang a mirror on the opposite wall. Avoid facing a blank wall; add an attractive landscape picture or other interesting image in front of the desk to avoid a feeling of being blocked in and prevented from achieving your goals.

Sha ch'i

Offices and studies are a dangerous place for the killing arrows created by angular furniture and open bookshelves. These will cut through the positive ch'i you have created and defuse its power. Choose glass-fronted bookcases or bookcases or cupboards with doors, if you can, so that reference materials, books and stationery are kept tidily out of the way. This will also help to settle your personal ch'i, as a chaotic and untidy room blocked with clutter will have a negative effect on your clarity of thought. Even if this is not possible, do make sure the room is kept tidy and clear of unnecessary rubbish. Deflect *sha ch'i* with mirrors or trailing plants.

Keep your desk tidy and place a crystal paperweight on the right-hand side to deflect any negative energies.

The Study Worksheet

Remember the feng shui principles repeated on pages 122–3 while you complete the worksheet on the study or office. You will also find additional useful information in the chapter on Feng Shui in the Workplace (see pages 178–84).

Room plan

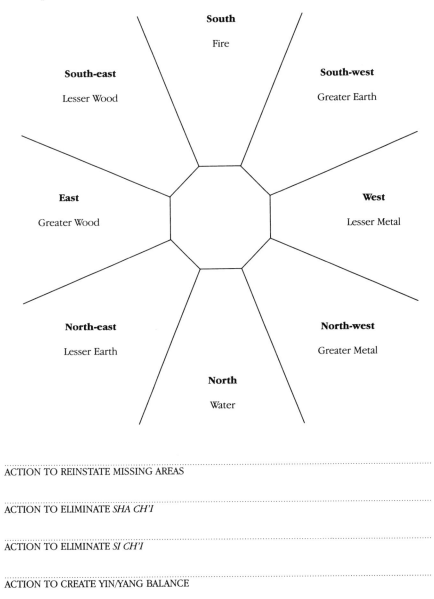

ACTION TO REINSTATE MISSING AREAS

ACTION TO ELIMINATE *SHA CH'I*

ACTION TO ELIMINATE *SI CH'I*

ACTION TO CREATE YIN/YANG BALANCE

ACTION TO RESTORE ELEMENTAL BALANCE

....

AREAS TO ENERGISE

....

....

ROOM MAINLY USED BY

....

MEMBER OF THE FAMILY

....

KUA NUMBER

....

ASTROLOGICAL SIGN

....

AUSPICIOUS DIRECTIONS

....

DIRECTION OF DESK

....

ACTION REQUIRED

....

....

....

....

....

....

....

....

CHAPTER 24

The Bathroom

The second main water room, the bathroom also relates to the family finances. Now that you have cleared your kitchen and made the energies auspicious, it is time to do the same in the bathroom.

The best bathroom positions are the east, which is good for the realisation of ambitions, and the south-east, which is good for communication. A bathroom in the northern zone of your home can over-emphasise the water element, especially if the kitchen is also in the north. Bathrooms positioned in the other compass sectors are also less auspicious. Reduce the potency of the water energies in the north by using browns and yellows and encouraging the wood symbolism, while reducing blues or black. Splashes of colour or the use of plants in the bathroom will be sufficient to redress the balance. Do the same in relation to the elements if the bathroom is positioned in other less auspicious sectors.

You can follow the same principles in considering the arrangement of the furniture of the bathroom itself. For example, if the sink or bath is in the north, you may want to add some plants or wooden elements to counter the strength of water.

Creating atmosphere

A bathroom does not need to be very large, but should not feel dark and cramped in case this same feeling applies to your finances. Use mirrors and plenty of light to give a feeling of spaciousness.

Using circular symbols of wealth and prosperity is good feng shui in the bathroom, so consider an oval or round bath if you have the space, and use round mirrors, shelves or other features.

Toilets

Since water relates to wealth and also to the flow of ch'i, the fact that the water in the toilet is regularly flushed away should make it clear that toilets need to be treated carefully in feng shui. Whatever zone of the house the toilet occupies, some of the qualities of that zone will be flushed away if the proper precautions are not taken. The best position for the toilet is therefore in the least auspicious direction of the main member of the household, or in an area where there is an excess of one energy which can afford to be counterbalanced. If that is not the case, stabilise the energies by placing a crystal or large stone as a feature in the room, otherwise the flushing away of positive energies in the south could lead to a poor reputation; in the north to a lack of career progress; in the east to bad health; in the west to a lack of joy and romance; in the north-east to poor motivation; in the north-west to a lack of responsibility; in the south-east to money problems; and in the south-west to poor marital relationships.

If toilets can be separate from the bathroom itself, this will help in keeping them as unobtrusive as possible. The toilet lid and the door of the room should always be kept closed, especially if the toilet is very near the main door or a bedroom door, as otherwise it will sour the ch'i as it enters the house and moves into the principal rooms. In this case, a mirror can be placed on the outside of the door to reflect the ch'i away, and this is also an auspicious move if the toilet is otherwise in a bad location.

Toilets bring a strong yin influence into their surroundings, so it may be necessary to introduce yang elements to counterbalance them.

A good circulation of air, and therefore of ch'i, is essential wherever the toilet is positioned, so a small window or air vent makes good sense.

The Bathroom Worksheet

Remember the feng shui principles repeated on pages 122–3 while you complete the worksheet on the bathroom.

Room plan

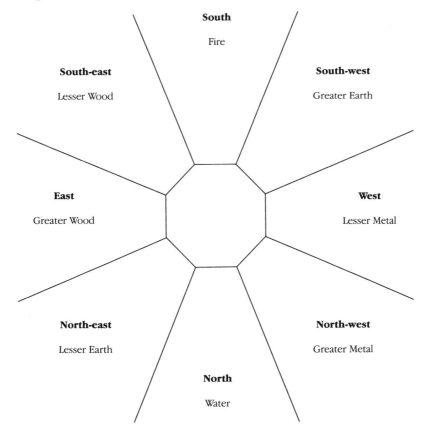

....
ACTION TO REINSTATE MISSING AREAS

....
ACTION TO ELIMINATE *SHA CH'I*

....
ACTION TO ELIMINATE *SI CH'I*

....
ACTION TO CREATE YIN/YANG BALANCE

....
ACTION TO RESTORE ELEMENTAL BALANCE

....
AREAS TO ENERGISE

CHAPTER 25

The Bedrooms

Bedrooms are an important place in feng shui as they are your personal refuge, the place where you recharge your bodily ch'i and where you go for total privacy and relaxation. If you are not restored by rest and sleep, you will not be able to perform your daily tasks. Bedrooms should therefore be carefully aligned with the correct feng shui energies, and also with your own personal energies so that they are most conducive to your personal freedom of expression.

Bedrooms in different sectors

The position of the bedrooms within the house has an effect on the ch'i energies within them.

North is ideal for quiet sleep as the zone has a calming energy which enhances spiritual depth. It is not good for those who are feeling lonely as it can lead to their becoming more isolated. The young and vibrant and those moving forward in their careers might also find this too relaxing a place to sleep. The north is associated with sex so is also a good place for the bedroom from this point of view.

The north-east has a sharp, motivating, competitive ch'i energy which can be too strong for bedrooms. It is certainly not suitable for anyone who is not already healthy or anyone who suffers from poor sleep, as it can even induce nightmares. Children sleeping in the north-east may exert too great an influence over the lives of their parents. Children are also best sleeping away from the north-western sector in case their influence becomes too strong. The north-west is the classic place for parents and for those in a stable phase of their lives where responsibility is the primary consideration.

The active and ambitious energies of the east are ideal for the young, especially if they are embarking on a new career. It will help them to realise their ambitions and have a forward-looking outlook on life. The second wood direction, the south-east, is also a positive position for those in business or developing a career, but the energies are more gentle and creative than those of the east, stressing communication as well as strong outward movement.

Those looking for passion should move their bedroom to the south, as this is the area which will stimulate their sex life. It is not the best position for sound sleep and relaxation! If the room is strongly red and the fire symbols are emphasised, the result could be insomnia and stress, so take care.

If you are looking for more pleasure and romance in your life, take the bedroom in the western zone to encourage greater contentment. As a down-side, you cannot expect it to stimulate your motivation or business progress at the same time, so make your choice.

The south-west is not the best direction for most people as the energies can be rather staid and create a feeling of caution. It is certainly not the best place for children's or young people's rooms. If you do have a bedroom in the south-west look closely at the room plan and stimulate the most appropriate areas for you.

Inauspicious positions for the bedroom

Those sleeping in bedrooms above a garage may find that their lives lack foundation. Stimulating the earth symbols in the room will give more support to their endeavours. It is also considered bad luck to sleep in a bedroom above a kitchen. If this is unavoidable, make sure the bed is not directly above the oven.

A bedroom in a basement will suffer from an excess of yin, associated with the earth and also with death. Add more yang to the room than you would normally expect to encourage in a bedroom.

If the staircase is directly confronting a bedroom door, hang a wind chime where the energies meet to moderate the flow, otherwise there may be an undesirable rush of energy into the room. It is not good feng shui if the bedroom door is immediately opposite the main door as this can indicate legal problems. Introduce an ornament or hang a wind chime to moderate the ch'i flow.

The shape of the room

Square earth shapes are the best for the bedroom as they are suitably yin. If the shape is irregular or there are areas missing from the room or alcoves which need activating, try to select other stimulators rather than mirrors to correct the problem. Hang a delicate wind chime on a protruding corner, for example. Built-in cupboards can also be used to regularise the shape of a room to good and practical effect.

Yin and yang

Clearly as a place of relaxation, yin should prevail, so softer colours, dimmer lighting, rounded shapes and soft furnishings find their home here. Only if you are waking unrefreshed and lethargic, or if your sex life needs stimulation, should you consider bringing more yang into the room. If you like some plants in the room, make sure they are round-leafed and do not include too many or the energies will be overactivated. Furniture should be more rounded than angular. Bedside tables must not direct sharp killing arrows at the sleepers, so must have rounded corners and be lower than the bed itself.

Personal auspicious directions

Try to find the best postion for the bedroom which relates personally to the occupant. If the room is not in the ideal place in the house, make the best selection you can, then support that by your positioning of the furniture in the room.

If is is possible to direct the head of the bed towards your best relationships direction, or a direction which is auspicious to both partners, this is the ideal. If not, make sure that it is not facing one of your worst directions. Placing the bed in the optimum sector of the room for you personally is also beneficial, although less important than the facing direction when sleeping.

Furniture placement and decoration

There are some other factors to consider which relate specifically to the position of the bed. Although the person in the bed should have a clear view of the door, they should not sleep with their feet pointing directly at the bedroom door; this indicates death, especially if the door leads to a bathroom or toilet, and this is not an issue on which you should compromise. Having your feet pointing directly at the window is considered bad luck; move the bed a little if you can. A bedroom should ideally only have one door, so that the ch'i can enter and circulate freely. If the room has two doors, there is a tendency for it to move too fast and be unable to accumulate. In this case, one door should be kept shut and you should try not to place the bed directly between two doors as it may be negatively affected by the ch'i movement. Either reposition the bed or use a decorative screen.

A solid wall behind the bed will offer support and security which will be lacking if the bed head is under a window. If you cannot avoid having the bed under a window, make sure you always close the curtains while you are asleep. Overhead beams directly above a bed are very bad ch'i and can even cause marriage breakdowns, so drastic measures may be called for. Move the bed to a better position or add a false ceiling. At the very least, move the bed as far as possible from the influence of the negative energies and hang two bamboo flutes at a forty-five degree angle by red ribbons on the beam.

Mirrors can be used to give a greater illusion of space or to increase the level of light, but be very careful where you place them to make sure they do not reflect the bed. The ch'i we give off while sleeping has a cleansing effect. If this cleansed energy is directed straight back at the sleeper, the effect will be much like breathing stale air. Mirrors here can also be harmful to personal relationships. If the dressing-table mirror reflects the bed, replace it with closing mirrors.

The shape of the headboard you choose can support your personality and lifestyle if you choose elemental shapes. Refer to the destructive elemental cycle (see page 45) to avoid the element which is negative to your own personal element. In addition to this, curved, metal-shaped headboards are good for office and business workers; rectangular wood-shaped headboards are auspicious for those in the professions; wave- or water-shaped headboards are best for creative types; triangular fire shapes are only suitable for anyone who does not want to get much sleep.

Subtle lighting will best enhance the yin qualities of relaxation and calm. This could be negated by a light hanging directly over the bed, which would be oppressive and cause the sleeper nervous problems. Similarly oppressive are shelves or cupboards around the head of the bed, a common problem with built-in furniture. This can create a blocking effect on your general good fortune. A calming effect will be achieved by placing six gold-coloured coins on each side of the bed.

Water features should generally be avoided in the bedroom as they have no auspicious tendencies in these circumstances and can indicate loss or burglary. Also, it is inadvisable to use any representations of the dragon in the bedroom. This ultimate symbol of yang is too strong an image where restful yin energies should predominate.

Improving your love life

If you want to activate your sex life, introduce more yang into the room with slightly brighter lighting and perhaps some music. Stimulate the southern part of the room with red, with candles and with a crystal hanging in the window.

If it is love and romance which are more on your mind, choose whether the south-western or western sectors are the appropriate areas to stimulate. The west relates to romance and joy. Enliven that sector with a candle or a red rose to encourage your romantic life. Stimulation in the south-west will help your marital or stable relationship. Try a picture of a pair of mandarin ducks in that zone, a Chinese symbol of true love.

Children's bedrooms

Although children still need to be refreshed by sleep, they will tend to play in their rooms as well as sleep so the balance will tip towards yang. Children's bedrooms are likely to be brighter and more alive, with music, posters and stronger colours. Take care that there is a balance and the strong energies do not prevent them from sleeping.

If they do their homework in the bedroom, apply the rules of auspicious direction to the position of their desk (see page 146). A good energy to enhance is that in the north-east. Hang a crystal in the window to catch the light and stimulate the energy of success. If they have a globe or a map of the world in the room, place this in the north-eastern sector, and support the elemental qualities of the room in the usual way. If the child has won metal trophies, display them in the west or north-west for added strength. Prize rosettes can be displayed according to their elemental colour.

Especially if they tend to be untidy, watch out for killing arrows which can destroy all the good ch'i you have established. Provide plenty of cupboard space, bookcases with doors and incentives (financial, perhaps!) for keeping the room clear of clutter.

The Main Bedroom Worksheet

Remember the feng shui principles repeated on pages 122–3 while you complete the worksheets on the various bedrooms in the house.

Room plan

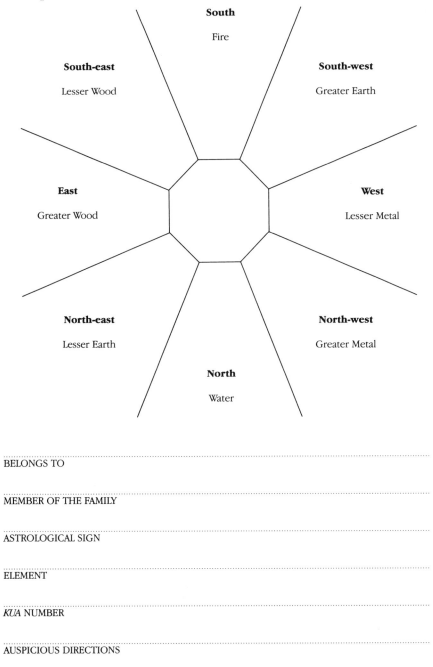

BELONGS TO

MEMBER OF THE FAMILY

ASTROLOGICAL SIGN

ELEMENT

KUA NUMBER

AUSPICIOUS DIRECTIONS

ACTION TO REINSTATE MISSING AREAS

ACTION TO ELIMINATE *SHA CH'I*

ACTION TO ELIMINATE *SI CH'I*

ACTION TO CREATE YIN/YANG BALANCE

ACTION TO RESTORE ELEMENTAL BALANCE

AREAS TO ENERGISE

Bedroom Worksheet

Room plan

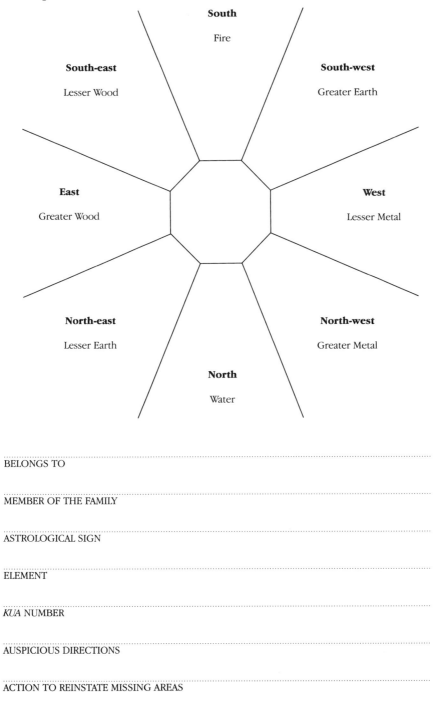

BELONGS TO

MEMBER OF THE FAMILY

ASTROLOGICAL SIGN

ELEMENT

KUA NUMBER

AUSPICIOUS DIRECTIONS

ACTION TO REINSTATE MISSING AREAS

ACTION TO ELIMINATE *SHA CH'I*

ACTION TO ELIMINATE *SI CH'I*

ACTION TO CREATE YIN/YANG BALANCE

ACTION TO RESTORE ELEMENTAL BALANCE

AREAS TO ENERGISE

CHAPTER 26

Other Rooms

Whichever room in the house you are working on, you can continue to follow the same principles when looking to improve your situation in life through feng shui.

The conservatory

A conservatory is generally not just a place in which to cultivate plants, but a valued room in the house in which you can relax and perhaps meditate. If it is spiritual stimulation you are seeking, the north of the house is the best position for a conservatory, but since this does not fit with the best position for horticulture, you may have to make a compromise. The south-east is an excellent position to encourage creativity and is a good alternative. A conservatory facing directly south may be overstimulated to the point where the passion in the house becomes aggressive.

A rounded shape is more strongly yin, so if relaxation is on your mind, this is a good choice. You may be using the conservatory as an office, playroom or games room which will be more active, however, in which case a more angular shape would create a better balance.

Plants in the conservatory will obviously be the best way to nourish and stimulate the ch'i, and you can focus the plants in particular zones if you want to encourage change in parts of your life or to stimulate the good fortune of a particular member of the family. The more plants you include in the room, the greater the shade you create, so keep balance in mind. Those with a penchant for cacti are unlikely to find it the most relaxing room in their home.

Workrooms and studios

Other kinds of workroom – such as sewing rooms or artists' studios – should, if possible, be in the western part of the house to encourage creativity, or the south-west, where they will be the most tranquil and practical. Again, yang energy needs to predominate in order to encourage activity and purpose, so good lighting and bright colours will work well. The place where the occupant works should be placed to align with one of their auspicious directions, if possible in the most relevant sector of the room. A view of the door is important for anyone sitting in a room, and can be achieved with a mirror if it is not possible actually to have the work station facing the door. Collections of rubbish are always bad feng shui, so regular cleaning and tidying is important.

Nurseries and playrooms

For tranquillity, place the nursery in the north; creativity will be encouraged in a playroom in the west; contentment should be found in the south-west. Ensure good energy flows through the room and try to keep it tidy; large cupboards in which toys can easily be stored when not in use will foster a good atmosphere. For a nursery, yin energies are the most suitable; for a playroom, yang should be stronger. A baby monitor placed in the eastern part of the room will stimulate contentment and good health.

Other Rooms Worksheet 1

Remember the feng shui principles repeated on pages 122–3 while you personalise and complete the worksheets on the various other rooms in the house.

Room plan

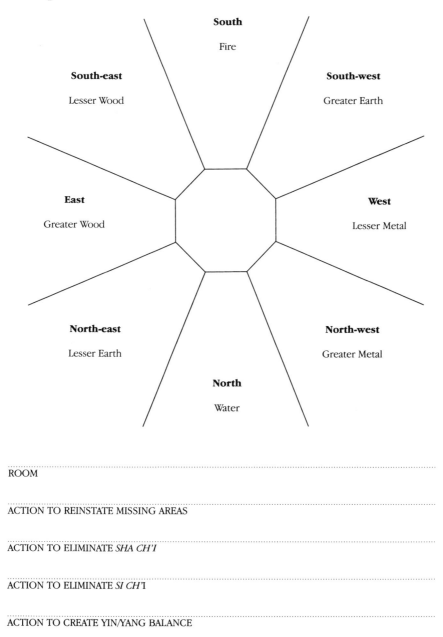

....
ROOM

....
ACTION TO REINSTATE MISSING AREAS

....
ACTION TO ELIMINATE *SHA CH'I*

....
ACTION TO ELIMINATE *SI CH'I*

....
ACTION TO CREATE YIN/YANG BALANCE

ACTION TO RESTORE ELEMENTAL BALANCE

AREAS TO ENERGISE

ROOM MAINLY USED BY

MEMBER OF THE FAMILY

ASTROLOGICAL SIGN

ELEMENT

KUA NUMBER

AUSPICIOUS DIRECTIONS

Other Rooms Worksheet 2

Room plan

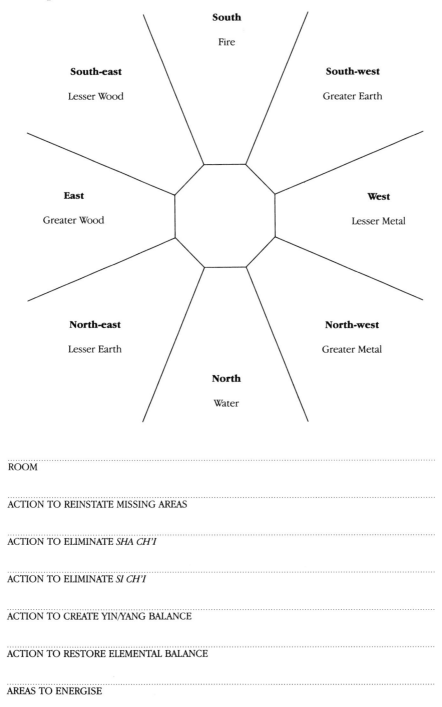

ROOM

ACTION TO REINSTATE MISSING AREAS

ACTION TO ELIMINATE *SHA CH'I*

ACTION TO ELIMINATE *SI CH'I*

ACTION TO CREATE YIN/YANG BALANCE

ACTION TO RESTORE ELEMENTAL BALANCE

AREAS TO ENERGISE

ROOM MAINLY USED BY

....

MEMBER OF THE FAMILY

....

ASTROLOGICAL SIGN

....

ELEMENT

....

KUA NUMBER

....

AUSPICIOUS DIRECTIONS

....

....

....

....

....

....

....

....

....

....

....

....

....

CHAPTER 27

Feng Shui in the Garden

Treat the garden as a room and use the same underlying feng shui principles in order to create the ideal feng shui garden. Remember that balance is all-important. A garden is a place where you will want both to be active and also to relax. How you achieve that balance and how it fits in with your own lifestyle is what you need to decide.

Celestial animals

The symbolic representation of the four celestial animals will already have been dealt with right at the beginning of your assessment of the form-school feng shui of your plot, so you may have already decided to plant trees, add fences or landscape other areas of your garden (see page 18). What you are aiming to achieve is a natural landscape – even if you have to give it a bit of help – with undulations and levels of interest, which represents the best arrangement of the dragon, tiger, turtle and phoenix.

The higher, dragon hills should be on the left of the house, with the lower, tiger hills on the right. A rounded hill, building or trees behind will add the support of the turtle, while a spacious area at the front leading to the footstool of the phoenix completes the picture. Ideally, the land behind the house should be higher than that at the front. If landscape features or buildings are not already in place, think about adding trees at the back or to the left of your house, with smaller shrubs to the right and an open area at the front. Do not make the mistake of planting too close to the house and overwhelming the property with shade. When you select a tree, look not just at its present size, but at how large it is likely to grow and how quickly. Fast-growing conifers, for example, may appear to provide a quick answer to a problem, but if they are not kept in check, they can swiftly become far too large for the house. Never block off all the natural sunlight coming into the house.

Levels in the garden

Dragons never live in completely flat land, so as well as gaining interest by having a garden with ups and downs, it is also more beneficial from the point of view of the luck which the plot can bring into your life. In addition, of course, it will help to create an auspicious circulation of ch'i, making sure that it does not rush across the garden without the chance to meander, settle and accumulate. Even if your plot is quite small, you can still artificially create small hills and hollows to encourage the ch'i to flow smoothly and calmly around the garden. Creating small hillocks, rockeries and so on will therefore have a beneficial effect from all points of view.

If the garden is very steep, however, this is too extreme and will cause the ch'i to move downhill too quickly. If you can, introduce terraces into the garden to encourage a slower and more beneficial flow.

The flow of ch'i in the garden plan

Make sure that you block off any killing arrows coming into the property from outside. You may be able to use fencing or trees, or add a trellis to the top of a fence and grow a trailing plant over it to deflect negative energies from outside. Use trailing plants to soften any harsh edges on the property or on sheds and garden buildings.

Think of the plan of your garden in the same way as you have been doing when placing your furniture in parts of a room. Rounded, flowing shapes are good feng shui. Sharp angles, large flat expanses, corners and swift changes of direction are not as auspicious. Tiny corners or pockets where the ch'i can stagnate will also cause you to lose the benefit of the energies in the garden. Make sure you encourage the ch'i to drift slowly but surely around the garden.

Think about the shapes rivers create as they meander down their course and introduce similar shapes into the garden. Even if you have a perfectly square, small garden, there is no reason simply to plant straight borders all round the edge. Be more interesting and inventive and you will automatically influence the atmosphere for the better.

It is best if you cannot view the whole garden at once, as if you can see right across the plot it must mean that there is nothing to direct the energies. When you are working out your planting scheme, remember that the heights of various trees and shrubs will make a big difference to the ch'i flow around the garden; taller trees or shrubs will act as more effective barriers, while lower-growing ground cover will have less of an effect. You can also use heights to help to add general interest. Introduce pergolas, screens, trellises or other features. Train trailing plants up the frameworks to soften the edges and create a beneficial effect.

Think always about the gentle breeze so that you can make an auspicious garden plan. Enliven or reshape areas which will collect *si ch'i*. Divert *sha ch'i* with rounded flower beds and water features. Introduce different heights with larger shrubs or trees, pergolas and trailing plants.

Curved pathways

Add interest to the garden and encourage the correct ch'i flow by creating curved pathways with bricks or stones. If you build a curved path on the eastern side of the house, this is said to activate the dragon to bring you good luck. Surround the path with flowering plants for added energies.

Yin and yang

A garden is alive and growing and the scene of family activity and enjoyment, but it is also a place where you will want to go to find peace and relaxation. As we have come to expect, therefore, you need a balance of light and dark, yin and yang.

Healthy, growing plants give off yang energy, while anything in the garden which is dead will give off yin energy. Make sure that you cut down and dispose of any dead trees or the stumps will create poison arrows in the garden. Tend the garden regularly to get rid of dead flower heads and leaves and generally to keep the garden looking tidy and healthy. Tangled undergrowth in the garden can confuse the ch'i as much as clutter in the house.

Plants with sharper leaves and lighter foliage, such as the bird of paradise plant, have more yang energy, while plants with rounded leaves have more yin. Yin plants will also prefer shaded or damper areas while the yang plants will prefer the bright sunlight. Look for a balance when you are planting, and focus yin-biased plants in the areas where you want to relax. Mix foliage colours and textures, shapes and heights for the best effects.

Overall there should be a balance of light and shade so that there is always somewhere you can sit in the sun, or a place where you can relax in the shade. A garden which is too bright is not relaxing but may become stressful; a garden which is always in shade has no upward-moving energy and will make you feel lethargic and apathetic rather than rested.

Types of plant

Plants with succulent or semi-succulent leaves which hold a store of water are highly auspicious in the feng shui garden.

A clump of bamboo signifies good health and longevity for the occupants of the house so is a good addition to the garden. Pine trees and other evergreens also symbolise longevity and many varieties have wonderful shapes and foliage colours to help in your garden planning.

Too many cacti or other plants with thorns are not good feng shui as they can create an atmosphere of aggression or tension. Avoid sharp-thorned hedging plants, such as pyracantha, too close to the house or you may suffer increasingly from stress. One positive way to use cactus plants is to plant two on either side of the front of the house. They are said to act as guardians to ward off evil spirits and protect against loss.

Weeping willows have connotations of death and should be well away from the house. They are not really ideal trees for a garden, especially a small one which would mean they are too near to the dwelling places of the living. Equally, two large trees blocking the front of the house resemble the incense burners placed in front of tombs and will chase away the yang energy. Replace them with smaller, flowering shrubs if you can.

Use creepers to soften sharp edges of buildings and prevent *sha ch'i* from cutting through your good luck. Don't let them take over and block out the sunlight from any of the windows; keep them well cut back. They should never be allowed to cover the house completely as this will strangle the energies of the house and could cause ill-health and bad luck for the residents.

Flowering plants

Fill your garden with flowering plants throughout as much of the year as possible. They really bring the energies of the garden to life. You can also use them to stimulate particular areas, in the same way as you have been doing in the house or in individual rooms.

Use the complementary elemental cycles to guide you in your choices of colour for specific zones. Red flowers in the southern zone will stimulate passionate energies and encourage your social life. If you are looking for a smoother career path, plant blue flowers in the northern sector, but enliven and strengthen it with white as well. Enhance your chances of romance by planting white flowers in the west, or improve your opportunities for realising your ambitions by enhancing the green colours in the east.

Another sense which can be activated by flowers is the sense of smell. This has wonderful emotional effects and can be very healing to personal ch'i. Choose from the huge range of fragrant plants – such as lilac, honeysuckle, gardenia, sweet pea, lily of the valley or fragrant roses – to plant near to the door of the house to make the most of their healing fragrances.

Herbs in the garden

Herbs can add fragrance, colour and a variety of leaf shapes to the garden. They are also useful in the kitchen and can be used for their medicinal properties. Used in cooking or as herbal teas, many herbs have health benefits and you can find many books on the subject in your library or bookshop.

The energies relating to the zones of the bagua are associated with different parts of the body (see page 70). If herbs are planted in the appropriate area of the garden, they can be most beneficial to that part of the body. Alternatively, you could create a herb garden planned out on a bagua pattern.

As well as planting herbs in the garden, feng shui also uses herbal aromas in the house. If you want to try this aspect of feng shui, always buy quality essential oils for the best results. Labelling requirements are not specific, so check when you are buying that the bottle contains pure essential oils, unadulterated with carrier oils. A few drops can be used in an oil burner, on a lamp ring, on a napkin or on the corner of a pillow.

Basil prefers to grow apart from other plants and is said to promote individuality and good fortune in personal ventures. Plant it in the northern area of the garden to encourage strength in your career. Do not use while pregnant.

Bergamot is an appetite suppressant and lifts the spirits. Plant it in the southern area to improve your standing amongst your friends or associates and make sure they are sincere.

Plant camomile in the west or south-west for good family relationships. A vase of freshly picked camomile in the east will help to calm those with nervous health problems, or they can be assuaged by a cup of camomile tea.

Dill is said to promote sleep. The northern zone is a good position for this plant.

Eucalyptus clears the head, either from head colds or muddled thinking. Plant it in the north-east to promote general clarity of thought and mental awareness. Mix fifteen drops each of eucalyptus oil and tea tree oil with a tablespoon of almond or other carrier oil and rub on to the scalp to clear head lice.

Jasmine can lift the spirits of those who are depressed and can also encourage good marital relations. Plant it in whichever sector of the garden needs stimulation: the east to help the health of the family; the south-west to improve family relationships; the south-east to encourage financial luck.

Plant juniper beneath bedroom windows to ensure marital happiness. Avoid the use of juniper when pregnant.

Lavender has many benefits. It makes a wonderful relaxant and aid to restful sleep, and can be used to help heal burns and soothe sunburn or irritated skin. It will benefit any area of the garden.

Mint promotes good memory and is refreshing. A good place to plant mint is in the north-eastern part of the garden to help in your search for knowledge or enlightenment.

Thyme should be planted in the south-eastern corner to promote wealth, or in the north to encourage a good career. In the home, it can be used to lift depression.

Rosemary is said to improve the memory. Plant it in the south-west to encourage remembrance between old friends. Do not use rosemary when pregnant.

Ponds and water

Ponds, waterfalls, streams, fountains, bird baths – all these can add good qualities to your garden. The best compass sectors for water features such as these are the north, south-east and east sectors of the plot, those related to water and wood. It is essential that the water remains clear and preferably flowing, as this will bring good luck. Stagnant or dirty water is not good feng shui.

A water feature in front of the house, in view of the main door, is good feng shui, as it mirrors the meandering stream in front of the perfectly placed feng shui dwelling.

If you are building a pond, choose a curved shape which relates to natural shapes and fits in with the general meandering nature of the garden. Kidney or crescent shapes, especially if they are curving towards the house, are very auspicious. If the shape curves away from the house, add some garden lights on the furthest points to redirect the energies back towards the house. Don't be tempted to make the pond too large for the proportions of the garden, otherwise you could find that you feel swamped by the water qualities you have created. If you already have a pond which you feel is too large, increase the light around it and add a rock garden or some boulders around it to rebalance the space.

Keep some fish in the pond, especially goldfish, choosing an odd number. Replace them if they die, as they will have absorbed your bad luck. Toads are also good luck so so they should be encouraged to live in your pond.

Because they create such a large expanse of water which is out of proportion to a normal home, swimming pools in private houses are not good feng shui. They can have the effect of overwhelming the house. If you are planning a pool, locate it in the north or in the lowest part of the plot. Try to screen it from the house with trees or shrubs so as to diminish any adverse effects.

Garden maintenance

Always keep larger trees and shrubs well pruned so that they remain the right size for the property and are healthy with evenly balanced growth. Plants which are brown or dying will give off excessive yin energy and damage the atmosphere you are trying to create, so keep everything in good order by regular maintenance. Sweep up leaves, especially in the autumn, so that they are not allowed to accumulate. Water features must also be clean and never allowed to stagnate.

Garden lighting

Apart from energising stagnant areas of the garden, lighting will add to your good luck, especially if it is placed around the boundaries of the plot. A light in the southern corner of the garden which is switched on for a few hours each day will bring good luck to the family by stimulating the fire zone. For stable and loving marital relationships, place a light in the south-west sector; to add to your romantic prospects, select the west.

Garden furniture and ornaments

By their very nature, gardens will usually be made up mainly of the wood element. Try to stimulate the other elements in your design in order to achieve more of the balance which is always desirable in feng shui. A square glass table with a metal base adds earth, water and metal. A white ceramic pot brings metal and earth. A blue wooden chair combines water and wood. All the elements can be added in this way.

If you have decorative statues, garden furniture, urns or planters to landscape your garden, think about the element from which they are made before placing them in an appropriate zone of the garden. Ceramic urns or pots of plants will bring you the best luck if they are placed in the earth sectors – south-west or north-east – or in the metal sectors – west or north-west. Wooden garden furniture will be best positioned in the east, south-west or south. This will also mean that it is most likely to catch the energising sun's rays to bolster your personal ch'i. Metal objects will be best in the west, north-west or north for their elemental properties to be most supportive.

Large boulders or rockeries can add stability to your luck if you feel that this is important in your life. Place them in the earth sectors – south-west or north-east – if you feel that your life is without foundation. For strength of purpose, place them in the west or north-west. Stones also add very strong yang energies to the garden, so be careful of your balance before you select anything too overpowering for the size of your garden. On a smaller scale, areas of raked gravel can add strength and interest.

Barbecues stimulate the fire element, so should be placed in compatible sectors: south, south-west or north-east.

The patio

Many people now have a patio at the back of the house which is where they sit and enjoy the garden, using the space to relax. You can apply the principles set out in this chapter and in earlier ones to the specific space of the patio, treating it as an individual room. The balance of yin and yang, for example, should probably be in favour of relaxing yin – unless, perhaps, you do a lot of entertaining. Since it is likely to be a stone base, increase the yin with subtle lighting and soft-leaved plants. Position your furniture to make the most of your own personal auspicious directions. Use colours to enhance the elemental qualities.

The Garden Worksheet

Remember the feng shui principles on pages 122–3 while you complete the worksheet on the garden.

Garden plan

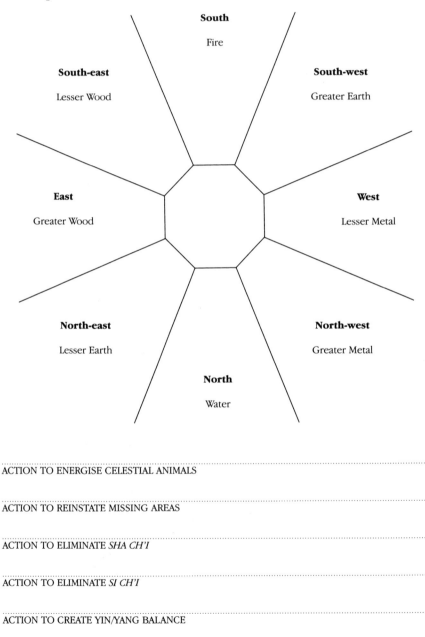

ACTION TO ENERGISE CELESTIAL ANIMALS

ACTION TO REINSTATE MISSING AREAS

ACTION TO ELIMINATE *SHA CH'I*

ACTION TO ELIMINATE *SI CH'I*

ACTION TO CREATE YIN/YANG BALANCE

ACTION TO RESTORE ELEMENTAL BALANCE

AREAS TO ENERGISE

WATER FEATURE

ACTION REQUIRED

PATIO

ACTION REQUIRED

CHAPTER 28

Feng Shui in the Workplace

You should now have a sufficient grasp of the principles of feng shui to understand that both the form-school principles and the bagua can be applied to any building – whatever its function – to assess its most auspicious qualities from a feng shui point of view and deal with any adverse influences. This is equally true of your workplace, whether it is an office, a studio or any other building.

If you are dealing with an entire building, you will need to go through all the relevant stages as you would with a house. The only difference will be that the balance of your thinking and the auspicious energies you are working to achieve will be slightly different. We will therefore go through the stages of the process in this chapter as a reminder, but the full detail will be found in the earlier chapters on the particular topics.

The four celestial animals and the external influences

The optimum position for any building reflects the support of the four celestial animals: the high hills of the dragon on the left; the low hills of the tiger on the right; rounded support from the turtle behind; and broad space with undulations at the front to symbolise the phoenix. Look back to the more detailed information on the four celestial animals on pages 18–27, which describes how to attain as close to an ideal arrangement as possible.

The flow of ch'i should ideally be steady and constant, neither rushing in a destructive fashion nor stagnating in corners. Killing arrows directed at the building by straight roads or angular structures will cut through and debilitate positive energies. Chapter 2 on pages 13–17 and chapter 4 on pages 29–35 discuss ch'i flow and how to optimise its beneficial effects.

The direction of the main door will influence the fortunes of the building and those working within it. Look back at pages 76–80 and apply the principles described there to the main door of your office building.

The floor plan and the arrangement of the offices

Deal with any compass zones which are missing from the floor plan in the same way as you would for a home (see pages 70–2).

By applying the bagua to the overall floor plan of the offices, you can assess the optimum positions for the members of the business depending on their particular skills and job responsibilities. Try to place managers in the north-western sector, creative workers in the east, those with financial responsibility in the south-east and human resources departments in the south-west. The optimum place for the managing director's office is in the heart of the building; it should certainly not be at the end of a long corridor, otherwise they will feel out of touch with the vital energies of the business. If the room has a high ceiling, all the better, as this gives an atmosphere of expansion and success.

If the arrangement of the offices is not as you would wish, look at the elemental qualities of the zones in which particular offices are placed and decide on how to stimulate the qualities which will be most useful to you (see pages 46–8).

The same principles apply when you are planning the arrangement and seating positions of the board room or a meeting room. If possible, the chairperson of the meeting should be in the north-west sector of the room and facing north-west to enhance their capabilities as a responsible and effective leader.

Yin and yang

Because an office is a place of activity, clearly it is important to ensure that the yang energies are stronger. In particular you should deal with yin energies imposing on the building from neighbouring empty buildings or areas associated with an excess of yin (see pages 38–40).

Inside the building, the best main colours are generally fairly neutral, as the level of electrical energy from active people, not to mention computers, printers, photocopiers, telephones and so on, will automatically mean that the atmosphere is yang. However, splashes of bright and lively colours in pictures or other smaller features are useful stimulation. Remember, though, that if there is a rest room or area where members of the company go to consider and discuss problems amongst themselves, that area should be more restful. If an office is too highly charged, it can become stressful and therefore a place of refuge to calm the personal energies is always beneficial.

The arrangement of furniture

Furniture arrangement within individual offices should follow the usual principles of aligning with the positive energies of the bagua (see pages 63–6) and with the most auspicious directions of the person using the space (see pages 103–5). Even if you cannot align the desk with the best direction, do try to avoid the worst ones.

Desks should not be placed so that the occupants have their back to the door, and they are best not positioned with their backs to the window, otherwise ch'i will enter through the door and go straight out through the window, missing any chance to settle and accumulate. If there is a window behind the desk, keep the blind closed while you are sitting at it. People sitting at desks too near to doors will find that their concentration is easily disturbed as they are too near to the change in the ch'i energies entering the room. In a home, a wind chime would moderate the flow, but if this is distracting, perhaps a plant may help. People working at desks too near the corner, especially if their chairs are actually in the corner of the room, will be influenced by slow-moving or possibly stagnant ch'i in the corner. Move the desks, or stimulate the ch'i with a crystal.

Interior decoration

A black desk may tend to slow you down, whereas wooden desks offer both support and growth potential. They should be comfortably large and neither too large for you to reach papers on the desk, nor so small that they create a feeling of cramped space and therefore bad personal ch'i. Square or rectangular desks offer the support of earth. Round or semi-circular desks are best for those in creative fields. Reflective surfaces or mirrors near the desk are bad feng shui as they apparently double the amount of work to be done. High piles of work will also be oppressive to personal ch'i. Keep your active paperwork to a minimum so that things are not allowed to pile up.

When you are using the telephone, make sure that the cable does not cross the work area and that you are able to sit straight while talking. If you bend your spine and sit with the phone cradled on your shoulder, your spine will not be straight and the flow of personal ch'i will be blocked. You will therefore not perform as effectively when doing business on the telephone.

Lights directly above the head are oppressive to personal ch'i and should be avoided; in fact, try to avoid anything hanging directly overhead as it will have a similar effect. If you cannot move the light, perhaps the desk can be moved slightly. Shelves above the desk also have this effect and are best avoided. Lighting generally should be bright but not harsh.

The colour of the office chairs can be used to stimulate or support the personal element of the person using them. You have already found your astrological sign and its associated personal element (see pages 97–101). Metal people should select a brown chair for support or a white one for strength. Water people will find a blue chair enhances their understanding or a white one will give them strength. A green chair will encourage the co-operative strengths of wood people, while a blue one will give them more understanding in dealings with other people. Red chairs will make fire people even more dynamic, although they may be better to choose green to help develop their ability to co-operate with others. Earth people will feel comfortable with the support of a brown earth chair, but may benefit more from the added dynamism of a fire-red chair.

The ideal picture to position on the wall behind the desk is one of a mountain to offer the support of the celestial turtle. Images which are abstract or too strong, however, will be a distraction and should be avoided or repositioned.

Directing the ch'i flow

Angular furniture, open bookshelves, filing cabinets, piles of work on desks and in trays – all these can create *sha ch'i* which cut through positive energies, and because of the nature of an office and the style of furniture, there are more likely to be killing arrows there than in the home. Be careful when positioning furniture, place plants to soften edges and use closed bookcases and cabinets.

Office furniture is generally square or rectangular, shapes which offer sound elemental qualities. If your office furniture features sharp angles or triangles, be especially carefully to balance these aggressive fire shapes and to avoid positioning the points to shoot directly at people sitting in the office.

Above all, keep the office as clear of clutter as possible. A well-organised

and tidy office fosters positive and structured thought and the ability to reason more clearly and effectively. Make sure the waste bin is not in the south-east – a bad position for a waste bin when the controlling energies are relevant to finances.

Plants are also a good way to stimulate areas of stagnant ch'i caused by a blocked-off section of the office if you are unable to rearrange the furniture to allow an easier flow of energies.

Stimulating specific areas

All the ways of stimulating energies which have been discussed can be used in the office. Think about elemental colours and symbols, lights, crystals, plants or mirrors. If working relationships amongst colleagues are troubled, stimulate the south-western zones. Energising the north-west will support and encourage the management team and strengthen their leadership qualities. Lack of creativity can be redressed by activating the western sector, while those looking for fame and recognition should look to the south. The finance sector, the south-east, should always be carefully examined and dealt with in any business.

In particular, the south-eastern sector, sometimes known as the 'fortunate blessings' sector, would benefit from a vase of fresh flowers.

The Workplace Worksheet

Remember the feng shui princples repeated on pages 122–3 while you complete the worksheet on the workplace.

Floor plan

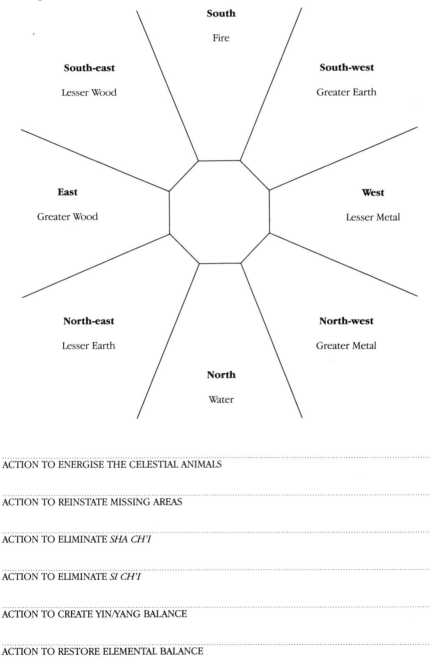

....
ACTION TO ENERGISE THE CELESTIAL ANIMALS

....
ACTION TO REINSTATE MISSING AREAS

....
ACTION TO ELIMINATE *SHA CH'I*

....
ACTION TO ELIMINATE *SI CH'I*

....
ACTION TO CREATE YIN/YANG BALANCE

....
ACTION TO RESTORE ELEMENTAL BALANCE

AREAS TO ENERGISE

PLACEMENT OF OFFICES

Office plan

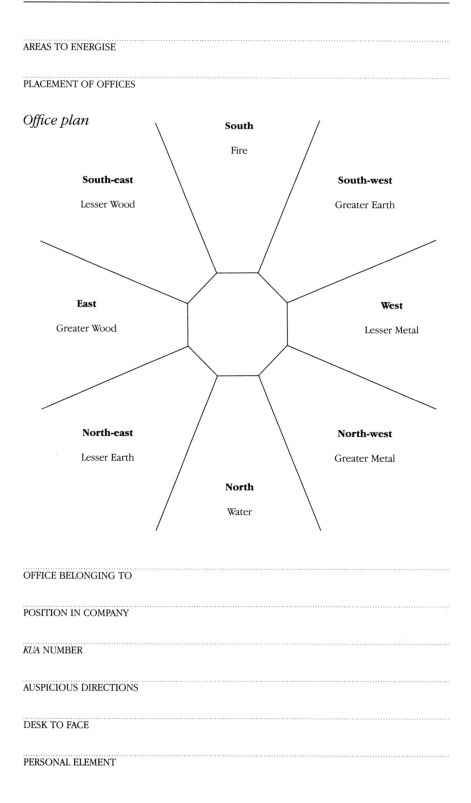

South
Fire

South-east
Lesser Wood

South-west
Greater Earth

East
Greater Wood

West
Lesser Metal

North-east
Lesser Earth

North-west
Greater Metal

North
Water

OFFICE BELONGING TO

POSITION IN COMPANY

KUA NUMBER

AUSPICIOUS DIRECTIONS

DESK TO FACE

PERSONAL ELEMENT

Glossary

You will find that some Chinese words may have different spellings in translation.

bagua	grid on which feng shui is based
ch'i	electromagnetic energy which flows through the universe
ch'ien	trigram relating to the north-west and the father
chai	the first, auspicious, measurement on the feng shui ruler
chakra	energy centre in the body
chen	trigram relating to the east and the eldest son
chieh	the sixth, inauspicious, measurement on the feng shui ruler
chueh ming	bad luck direction
chu-shr	mystical solutions
fu wei	personal growth direction
hai	the seventh, inauspicious, measurement on the feng shui ruler
ho hai	accidents direction
hseuh	ideal home site
hsing	the five moving agents; the elements
hsun	trigram relating to the south-east and the eldest daughter
k'an	trigram relating to the north and the middle son
k'un	trigram relating to the south-west and the mother
ken	trigram relating to the north-east and the youngest son
kou	the mouth of the home; the main door
kua number	lucky number
kwan	the fifth, auspicious, measurement on the feng shui ruler
li	the third, inauspicious, measurement on the feng shui ruler
li	trigram relating to the south and the middle daughter
lo pan	feng shui compass
lo shu	magic square

lui sha	worst luck direction
nien yen	relationships direction
pa kua	*see* bagua
pi	the second, inauspicious, measurement on the feng shui ruler
pun	the eighth, auspicious, measurement on the feng shui ruler
ren ch'i	ch'i moving through the wind and water
ren chai	mankind luck which you create for yourself
ren choy	see *ren chai*
ru-shr	logical solutions
sha ch'i	fast-moving and destructive energies
shakra	*see* chakra
sheng ch'i	the ideal movement of energies and best luck direction
si ch'i	stagnant energies
ti ch'i	ch'i moving through the landscape and the environment
ti chai	earth luck which can be influenced by feng shui
ti choy	see *ti chai*
tien ch'i	heaven ch'i over which you have no control
tien chai	heavenly luck over which you have no control
tien choy	see *tien chai*
tien yi	good health direction
trigram	three-line symbol denoting a balance of yin and yang
tao	the interaction of yin and yang which is the basic principle of the universe
tui	trigram relating to the west and the youngest daughter
wu kwei	quarrels direction
yang	the male, bright side of the energies of the universe
yi	the fourth, auspicious, measurement on the feng shui ruler
yin	the feminine, dark side of the energies of the universe

Index